WHEN AIDS COMES HOME

WHEN AIDS COMES HOME!

The true story of how a transfusion of
AIDS contaminated blood brought a
Christian family to deal with the
ultimate nightmare.

By
Wayne Marshall
(alias Jerry Thacker)

SCEPTER PUBLICATIONS

BOX 265, MORGANTOWN, PA 19543
610-286-7744

Unless otherwise noted, Scripture quotations are from the
New American Standard Bible,© the Lockman Foundation
1960, 1962, 1963, 1968, 1971, 1972,
1973, 1975, 1977.

ISBN: 0-89957-102-6

Printed the United States of America

To my Wife and Children,
my Brother and Sister-in-Law,
and all the Christian families
whom this malady will touch. For all of us,
AIDS is not an abstraction,
but a reality brought into our lives by a loving
Heavenly Father who intends all our
circumstances to work out for our ultimate good
and His glory (Romans 8:28)

Contents

Preface

Wayne Marshall is not my real name. I'm the guy next door or the guy in the pew next to you. I'm someone you know who right now is carrying the AIDS virus and doesn't know it. How will you react to me when you find out I have AIDS? That's what this book is all about.

My purpose in writing this book is to help you understand several things: (1) AIDS is not necessarily a homosexual's disease. You could contract it the same way my wife and I have. (2) We may be your next door neighbors. Most people who are HIV infected aren't going to broadcast it—there's too much to lose. (3) We may be sitting next to you in church. I'm not trying to make you paranoid, but you need to know that within the next five years, three out of every ten people in your acquaintance will know someone like us.

Now is the time to sort out what you believe and how you feel about AIDS as a disease and about people with AIDS—whether they are homosexuals, drug addicts, fornicators, or people like us, who have not participated in such activities, but have nevertheless contracted the AIDS virus. It's also time for you to help your church come to grips with the need to minister to these folks in a caring and compassionate way.

I have hesitated in finishing this material to a stage in which it could be published because, in some ways, I have believed that finishing it would perhaps lead the

Lord to take me home at its completion. But the burden I feel to get out the message and perhaps increase the understanding of those who name the name of Christ as Savior is greater than I can stand. The message contained in this book needs to be disseminated far and wide among God's people. Perhaps it will help them prepare for what is coming.

At this time, I am convinced that a major AIDS–related crisis is coming to the country and to our churches. It will challenge our healthcare system as its resources are diverted to take care of the dying. It will also test the mettle of all who believe in the Lord and claim to have experienced His love and compassion toward them. It will require that each Christian come to his own conclusions about how he will react the first time he finds out that a close friend, relative, or business acquaintance is HIV positive or dying of full–blown AIDS.

It is my prayer that this book will help you think through your reaction to the coming epidemic and arrive at the conclusion that you will show the love of Christ to all whom this disease will touch. The opportunity to advance the cause of Christ and show forth His love to dying men and women is coming. I'm sure that it will also be a time when some will show their callousness and hardness of heart as they react selfishly and in a non–Christian manner.

Please read this book carefully and try to place yourself in the same situation. How would you feel? How would you react? Please pray through your attitudes as you finish each chapter.

How will you react when you find out that someone you are close to has AIDS? How will your church react? How will you choose to minister to these needy folks who are physically—and perhaps spiritually—dying?

That's what this book is all about.

May God bless you and help you read with an open heart and mind. And may he keep us all safely in His love.

Fall 1991

1

September 1986—The Nightmare Begins

O may Thy lovingkindness comfort me, according to Thy word to Thy servant. May Thy compassion come to me that I may live, for Thy law is my delight.—Psalm 119:76, 77

It was just a little past five in the morning on a Saturday when I slid behind the wheel of my new car and started to the office. The early fall air had a bit of a chill in it.

The business has its crazy times, especially in the fall, and I'd been pushing too hard for the past several weeks. As I traveled toward the office from our family's suburban home, I was a bit nauseous because I was tired and had been working more than seventy hours a week. However, regardless of my physical state, my best

1

mental time is the early morning. It's also a time when no one else is at the office and the phone doesn't ring. By going in early on Saturday morning, I can often get the equivalent of a regular day's work done in three hours and then go back home to spend some much needed time with the wife and kids.

When I got to the office, I started clearing away the debris that had collected on my desk from the previous day. I had been in another part of the state engaged in the seemingly endless search for new business. On the left side of the desk was a financial report on one of our companies. There was some correspondence that needed to be reviewed, and there were the usual pink slip phone messages. Call this client. A salesman called. Call your wife—I had already handled that one in person. Then there was a different one . . . from a doctor I didn't know at the local blood bank.

Ten days earlier I had volunteered to give blood. Our church, being the civic–minded organization that it is, has the blood–bank people come to collect at our social hall. My wife had signed me up. It was the first time I had ever given blood. Due to an anti–hypertensive drug I was previously taking, I had not been able to give before. And I wanted to give now because the blood bank had been good to us. When my daughter was born, two and one–half years earlier, my wife had required four units of blood. When my five–year–old son had a serious accident, another four units had been needed. It was simply smart to give blood for the insurance of my family's blood supply as well as to help others. Who knows when any of us will need to make a withdrawal.

The phone message said that I was to call the doctor on Monday, but if I wanted to call him at home on

Saturday or Sunday, I could. That last part made an alarm go off inside me. Most doctors stopped making house calls long ago and they have answering services that take their calls. They don't want you to call them at home. In fact, none that I've ever known had ever asked me to call them at home. I knew something was dreadfully wrong.

I had been out of the country on a trip to visit some missionaries the previous year. Perhaps I had picked up some rare foreign blood disease. Perhaps some alien "bug" had found its way into my blood stream.

Then I remembered that the blood donation volunteers had given me a paper on HIV (human immunodeficiency virus) screening. At the time, I read it quickly and dismissed it. After all, AIDS is something that homosexuals and drug users get, not monogamous Bible–believing Christians. I didn't even know any homosexuals or drug users. And the only person in the entire world I'd had sexual contact with was my wife.

Until 9:00 a.m. I went through the hollow motions of my work. I read the reports, wrote memos, and even went for a haircut. I tried to keep my mind off the situation, but the nagging thought came again and again, "What if you have AIDS?"

In my mind I reasoned that it couldn't be. Why would a loving God let one of His children get something that most preachers have equated with the sins of Sodom and Gomorrah? Why would God let this come into my life now, just when the job was going so well and my family was growing up so very nicely?

A little after 9:00 a.m., I picked up the phone and dialed the doctor's number. A woman answered and I could hear several small children in the background.

The doctor's house sounded like mine. There's something about kids under five that makes them always noisy. But I suppose it beats the stillness of an empty house devoid of such life–filled noisemakers.

The doctor's voice was professional. He first wanted to make sure that he had the right guy. He asked where the blood had been given and if I'd ever given before. I told him that this was my first time and gave him the reason why. Then these burning words seared my consciousness, "Your HIV test came back positive."

Immediately my body gave a boost of adrenaline that made my heartbeat quicken as fear shot through to my very soul. My mind started racing through a thousand possibilities and the stored pictures of scores of TV news reports. I saw grotesque, emaciated figures covered with hideous skin eruptions. I saw bearded, bald, and thin remainders of men waiting for an ignominious death. I saw my three beautiful children fatherless outcasts unable to attend church or school.

Then I had a natural, normal thought. I thought that it must be a terrible mistake. Surely some horrible plot of Satan was responsible for this awful news. Surely some unwitting lab assistant had mixed up the blood samples.

I asked the doctor if a positive test was common. The answer was an unqualified no. In more than eight thousand local tests of blood donors, only two had ever turned up positive. "Surely the samples were mixed up," I responded. The doctor's reply was clear and controlled. "We'd like to repeat the test," he said.

"Where and when?" I responded. I wanted to get this over with as quickly as possible and get on with my life. "Meet me at my house at 9:30," came the reply.

The doctor lived in a nicer part of town as doctors usually do. His house was a lot like mine—nice, upper middle class, pleasant. As I walked up to the door, I found myself not believing this was happening. Why was I here? How did I pick up the virus if I indeed had? What happens next?

One of my favorite phrases has always been that great statement by a missionary, "The future is as bright as the promises of God," but right now, from a purely physical standpoint, it looked quite bleak.

The doctor was about my age, in his mid–30s, thin, and professional. He quickly explained to me that a positive HIV test is not an indicator of AIDS. In fact, at that time there was no test available to determine if the AIDS virus was actually present. The HIV procedure does, however, prove the presence of an antibody to the AIDS virus. In this way it indicates that the person has been exposed to the virus at sometime in the past.

The doctor asked questions one would expect from the man who is in charge of supervising a community blood bank. Any drug use? No. Any blood transfusions? None for me, but yes, my wife had 4 units at the birth of our last child. Any homosexuality? No. Multiple sexual partners? No, just one in my entire life.

How happy I was to be able to tell him that my wife and I had been pure as teens and that there had been no extra–marital sex in our lives together. God had preserved us from these sins through the years, and now that our lifestyle was indeed under microscopic scrutiny, I was glad for His preserving and keeping.

"The test results will be back Wednesday," the doctor said after drawing about two tablespoons of blood into a vacuum tube. "Call my office then for the results.

If they're positive, we'll want to get them verified by several other labs and then get your wife tested, too."

I went back to the office but found I couldn't work at all. My mind flitted to a thousand things—things like life insurance, and disability insurance, schooling for my kids. What would my wife do in case of my untimely death? What would happen to the children if we both died? What would happen to the business I had spent years building? Then the obvious thought Christians have when things look bleak came—how great it would be for the Lord to come today and end this entire mess!

My wife and I have always had a good relationship. Why shouldn't we? The Lord gave us to each other while we were in Christian college. He made us for one another, and we've always been able to talk about anything—good or bad. I decided I couldn't hold this from her. I called and told her about the test results. Her reaction was just as I knew it would be. First, there was total disbelief in the test and its results, followed by her pledge to stick by me to the very end regardless of when that would be or from what cause.

You see, my wife and I have both known the hurt of dying and death. First it came with the death of my grandfather, who was like a father to me. Then my father died suddenly of a heart attack. He was just in his mid–50's. After all these years, I still miss him desperately. Most recently, my wife's father had died.

Yes, we understand the pangs of grief to a certain extent. We also know that life and death are both great imposters to the Christian. God has given us eternal life that no one can snatch away. It is our present possession as members of "the forever generation." If one of us dies before the other, the waiting time for our reunion will be very brief, and no time at all in the sight of God.

As I drove home from the office, I was in shock. But if there has been one thing that I have learned as a business executive it is that there is more to any story than what the public press presents. I was determined to find out more about the test. What did a positive result mean? How long would I live if I indeed had AIDS? Given the current feelings associated with the subject, how could I do the research and not let anyone know?

After several hours of letting the news sink in, I knew I had to talk to someone else. Someone I could trust. Someone who could help me understand what I should do next. Even just someone who could help lift me up at a time when the props had been knocked right out from under me. My first thought was to see our pastor, but for some reason, I quickly dismissed that idea. Ten days later I would know why the Lord impressed me that way. While I love our pastor dearly, he is a hard man to get to know. I know he cares for us deeply, but I still did not feel I should talk with him.

Our associate pastor is a trained nouthetic counselor. He has a regular full-time counseling practice and has handled about any problem people can have. He is also a close personal friend with whom I share many characteristics. As the Lord would have it, I found him at the church on this Saturday morning. When I stuck my head in his door and announced, "I need to talk to you," he could tell by the expression on my face that something very serious was bothering me.

In many ways he is like a brother to me. He is about the same height, and he has faced some of the same besetting sins I have in my life. We've always been able to talk freely about anything, and his counsel is kind, sometimes firm, and always wise.

Somehow I didn't feel that even the walls of the church should hear what I had to discuss with him, so we drove to a nearby lake. It was a beautiful day with a brisk fall breeze and sunshine. The lake was an idyllic setting on such days, but the heaviness of the problems at hand somehow seemed to mute the brightness of God's creation at that hour.

My associate pastor–friend's first reaction as I shared the news was complete shock and surprise. I think that in his mind he knew that something like this would come up someday. The sin of a society and the results of that sin always affect those who never participate in the sin. Just as it is certain that drunken drivers will sometimes kill innocent non–drinkers, so the diseases which seem to be a by–product of those who pervert God's natural plan will find their way to those who don't. Even "righteous Lot" was affected by the sin of his day. While we might question his judgment in living in a place like Sodom, God still allowed the sin of the people to affect His man.

Having attended counseling classes taught by my friend, I knew the questions that were obviously running through his mind. The first one was, "Am I being told the truth about this person's sexual conduct?" We have both seen enough in our lives to make us "pastoral realists." We understand that there is no sin which has ever been committed that we could not ourselves commit under the proper provocation. So I answered the question before it was asked. No, there had been no promiscuity in our family. But, yes, there had been blood transfusions. The answer satisfied him. The fact that he had known me for years backed my words with a history of my involvement in the work of our church and my desire to serve the Lord with my life.

I believe that Christians should live transparent lifestyles, that is, that they should be the same at work, at home, and at church. But sometimes I think we're too transparent for our own good. For instance, sometimes when my associate pastor–friend looked at me, I was obviously struggling with a load of care. As he put it, my "halo data was not too good." Well, this piece of information was about the heaviest burden I had had to bear in years. But it was time to put on a mask of "all's well," until I could find out more. How hard that would be for one whose entire life had been open and straightforward. However, one does what is necessary at times like this. So I determined to find out as much as I could about the possible situation I was facing. As I went back home still very much in shock, I prayed and asked the Lord to help me through this experience.

I remembered being with my grandfather on his deathbed. The cancer was destroying his liver and his lungs were filling with fluid. I held his hand and told him there was only one way through this situation— and that was to go straight through it to whatever God had next. In his case it was a home in heaven. In mine that would be the case too, but how much of earth and its cares would I face in the meantime?

Lord, I don't know what's coming now, but I know you're in control. Help me to be faithful and to trust in you I pray.

2

We Find Out More

If Thy law had not been my delight, then I would have perished in my affliction. I will never forget Thy precepts, for by them Thou hast revived me. I am Thine, save me; for I have sought Thy precepts.—Psalm 119:92–94

Computers are both my hobby and a tool for my work. I write a great deal as a part of my vocational calling. As a computer enthusiast I like to find out what is available in the expansive world of information databases. It is possible to find out just about anything you want with a computer. There are on–line encyclopedias and medical libraries and even special interest groups that share information, and grass–roots rumors, on almost any topic imaginable.

To find out more about the HIV test and what it meant, I spent that Saturday afternoon checking into several computer databases. First there was the general information about AIDS that I was able to find on the database put out by the U.S. Department of Health and Human Services. It's in the form of a question and answer discussion of the subject. Here are some of the things I found out.

AIDS is not a specific disease, but an entire sequence of illnesses that the body doesn't fight off because of a defect in the immune system. Apparently people who suffer from it become susceptible to a variety of rare illnesses called "opportunistic diseases." In most normal people, cases of these diseases are rather mild. Our God–given immune system wards them off constantly and well. Even starting cancers can be destroyed by our immune system. In the AIDS patient, however, these diseases become severe and even lead to death as the immune system malfunctions in a major way.

The two most common diseases the syndrome leaves one open to are Pneumocystis Carinii Pneumonia and Kaposi's sarcoma, a rare form of cancer or tumor of the blood vessel walls.

Those who have contracted the syndrome recall symptoms like: fever, night sweats, swollen glands (enlarged lymph nodes)—in the neck, armpits, or groin—unexplained weight loss, yeast infections, diarrhea, persistent coughs, fatigue, and loss of appetite.

It is also interesting to note that almost all of the AIDS cases have occurred in people belonging to one of several distinct groups:

    ** Sexually active homosexual and bisexual men with multiple sex partners. (This group accounts for more than 70 percent of all reported cases);

    ** Present or past abusers of intravenous drugs, 17 percent;

    ** Hemophiliacs, 0.7 percent.

These groups all left me out although I'm sure that I would not want to be included in any of them. Then how was I exposed? How does anyone get exposed? According to the database information, I found that there are only two ways.

AIDS appears to be transmitted primarily through sexual contact or through blood from a person who has AIDS. Most of the cases have been in homosexual and bisexual men with multiple sex partners.

I thought that this left me out, too. I've had only one sexual partner in my life, and I've been happily married to her for many years. But there was more.

AIDS has also been found in intravenous drug abusers, leading investigators to suspect that AIDS is transmitted by blood on contaminated needles that have been shared.

That wasn't me either. Aside from an occasional prescription given to me by the doctor, an aspirin is about the strongest drug I've ever taken. Even though I grew up in the late 60's when drug experimentation was the thing to do, my association with Bible–believing churches and Christian ministries had pretty much kept me on the straight and narrow path. I had never "done" drugs.

Other evidence for transmission of AIDS through blood products was found in the occurrence of AIDS in hemophilia patients receiving large amounts of Factor VIII, a clotting substance in blood.

There was no hemophilia in our household, but wait. There were those blood transfusions when my wife delivered our last child. In fact, she required four units of blood due to "weeping" while they were repairing her womb and abdominal tissues after her "C–section." I remember the nurses running down the hallway at three o'clock in the morning with bags of blood in their hands. Perhaps that's the connection.

But wait a minute. If that is indeed the way I contracted the virus—through my wife—then we've both probably been carrying around the virus since 1984. It hasn't killed us yet. Nor has it killed anyone around us. At least that much was a comfort.

To read accounts in the mass media, you would think that a person in the same galaxy as someone with the virus would become infected. The database shed a little light on this too:

> No cases have been found where AIDS has been transmitted by casual contact with AIDS patients or persons in the high risk groups. Ambulance drivers, policemen, and firemen who have assisted AIDS patients have not become ill. Nurses, doctors, and other health care personnel have not developed AIDS from exposure to AIDS patients.

This was all fine and good. But it still had not answered my questions about the HIV test itself. What does a positive result mean? I decided to dig deeper into the data.

The state of California has been first in a lot of areas. Many of the things the rest of the nation has obtained from the folks on the west coast are of questionable value—things like drug experimentation, loose morals, fad fashions, etc. But in some areas, California has led the way in the collection of information and the addressing of problems concerning public health. This is true of AIDS.

My research showed that a complete treatise on the meaning of a positive HIV test had already been developed by the California Department of Public Health. The information was encouraging. Here are some of the findings:

> 1. The HIV antibody test is not a test to diagnose Acquired Immunodeficiency Syndrome (AIDS), but may be of assistance in confirming the diagnosis, especially in a person with no

known risk of exposure to AIDS. The test can distinguish whether someone in a high risk group has or has not been infected with the HIV virus.

2. The HIV antibody test is a useful tool that can assist in protecting the nation's blood supply, and is a valuable test to assist research efforts into the AIDS problem.

3. At the present time, the HIV antibody test is not recommended for any purposes other than those stated above. The HIV test should not be used for generalized screening or as a precondition for employment, evidence of insurability, or admission to school or the military.

4. Because of the serious potential for harm to the individual resulting from misinterpretation of the HIV antibody test results, great care must be taken to inform the public and health care professionals about the limitations in current understanding of the test results and of the entire disease process labeled Acquired Immunodeficiency Syndrome.

5. Information gathered from the testing or counseling of individuals should be kept strictly confidential.

6. State and local health departments, working in concert with the private medical and hospital communities, university systems, blood banks and plasma centers should establish a network and referral system (where not previously established) of physicians and other health care providers with expertise in dealing with AIDS.

7. Currently, there is limited availability of tests to detect the virus itself. In the absence of such tests, it is useful to determine whether there is any clinical or epidemiologic evidence of exposure to HIV (i.e., is the individual in an "at–risk" or "high–risk" group). If so, the predictive value of the positive result (or the likelihood that the positive result truly represents infection with HIV) may be about 99%. When such clinical or epidemiologic evidence is lacking ("low–risk"), interpretation of test results is even more difficult and the predictive value of a positive test may be less than ten percent. In the later circumstance, much attention must be paid to seeking or excluding additional evidence of infection, including confirmatory serological testing, virus isolation (if possible), and evidence for spread to or from regular sexual partners.

At least now I was getting somewhere. Apparently, the HIV test is not a test for the presence of the virus itself, but simply acknowledges the presence of antibodies to the virus showing that an exposure has taken place at some time.

The fact that I was still alive lent some credence to the theory that the test may be wrong. But there was not enough data to make that judgment immediately.

As I went from my computer terminal to the outdoors to cut the grass, I thought about how good God is in letting us live each day. The old Puritans used to pray each morning and thank the Lord for His, "watch-care through the night." They were quite right in doing that. In Him we live and move and have our being, and it is only by His mercy that we are not consumed by war, pestilence and death.

As I put my lawn mower through its paces, the words of a song came to mind:

> *Every joy or trial falleth from above*
> *Traced upon our dial by the Son of*
> *love.*
> *We may trust him fully all for us to do*
> *Those who trust Him wholly find Him*
> *wholly true.*
> *Stayed upon Jehovah hearts are fully*
> *blessed*
> *Finding as He promised perfect peace*
> *and rest.*
> —Frances R. Havergal

3

Getting Alone With God

Remember the word to Thy servant, in which Thou hast made me hope. This is my comfort in my affliction, that Thy word has revived me.—Psalm 119:49, 50

When you're a kid, it seems time never moves fast enough. I felt the same way waiting for Wednesday to come and with it the results of the confirmatory tests. For three days I prayed that I would hear that the lab had mixed up the samples. I hoped the nightmare would die as quickly as it had been born on Saturday morning. But somehow, in the back of my mind, I knew it wouldn't. Somehow I knew that God wanted to do something special in my life and that this experience was the next step in building that "proven character" spoken about in the Scripture and developed as a part of the tribulation process.

My business takes me out of town for several days at a time each month. This time I dreaded the trip because of the heaviness of the cloud I felt over me. Obviously, no one knew the turmoil going on inside me. No one knew the doubts and fears that were bundled in my heart because of the terror of the unknown weighing heavily upon me. But I went on my trip anyway believing that God would help me come to an understanding of what He was trying to do in my life.

The Book of Job has never been one of my favorites, probably because I've never had to suffer much in this life. But somehow I felt that I needed to read about this remarkable man in preparation for what might be coming.

It is my habit to keep a diary where I summarize what I have been studying in my devotions, and my Bible study diary for those days became one of my primary ways of keeping things in perspective. In the quietness of being alone and a thousand miles from home I wrote:

> Job's life is an example for all of us in focusing on the purposes of suffering and on what is really important. Chapter one ends with a statement of principle which puts all that we have and are in perspective—
>
> > Naked I came from my mother's
> > womb
> > And naked I shall return there.
> > The LORD gave and the LORD has
> > taken away.
> > Blessed be the name of the LORD.
> > —Job 1:21

These two thoughts sum up all that we need to know about life and death. Job had just suffered the loss of all his riches and all his ten children. He was probably in the shock that comes from bearing up under such tragic losses, yet his immediate response was to recognize where all his "good things" and all these people came from. They were gifts from God.

In this one statement we see Job's belief in God's Sovereignty, God's Providence, and God's continuing care. We see an eye that looks heavenward toward eternity, and a spirit that knows that even his own physical existence depends upon God.

As Christians, we give mental assent to the fact that God holds all things together. But when they come apart, our humanity sometimes makes us waver in that persuasion. During these doubtful days I was so glad that the Scriptures were there to comfort me. The eternal perspective is always bright for one who knows that this life is but a vapor after which there are joys eternal and full of glory.

In the quietness of being alone in my hotel room, I thought of the three deaths we had experienced in our church in the past two months. Two were young people, much younger than I. The other was an old man whose Christian family and kindness were his legacy.

The death of the youths seemed a great tragedy. One had committed suicide. What do you say in such a case? The despair apparently outweighed the joy of living for the young man.

The other had been a boy I had taught in Sunday school class. Only in the past year had he really gotten close to the Lord and deeply involved in God's work. His end was at a good time in his life. Perhaps the Lord took him home to keep him from wandering later on.

As I thought on these things, I reviewed my own life and accomplishments for God. I'm thankful he saved me out of a non–Christian home just before my teenage years. He led me to a fine Christian college where I was able to serve for many years. I'd been able to preach to tens of thousands through my involvement in outreach ministries. He had given me a wonderful wife who loves Him first and me next. And he had blessed us with three beautiful children with tender, sensitive spirits that want to do what's right.

My work had allowed me to have an effect on companies that contribute millions of dollars to the Lord's work and to be involved in the molding of ministries that will have an effect on Christian people for scores of years. It would be a good time to die if that is what the Lord would want. Sometimes I get so tired of the fight with remaining corruption. It seems I make so little progress.

In a way I was dreading Wednesday morning. In a way I knew what would come. The words of Job put it all in the proper perspective. He wrote:

Shall we indeed accept good from God and not accept adversity? . . . (Job 2:10b).

4

A Rough Wednesday

Deal bountifully with Thy servant, that I may live and keep Thy word. Open my eyes, that I may behold wonderful things from Thy law.—Psalm 119:17, 18

As I arrived at my office on Wednesday morning, I felt I already knew the results of the test. Somehow the carefulness of the volunteers who helped draw the blood when I donated at the church had made me feel that a sample mix–up was almost impossible. I also knew that the sample they were now testing was not from that batch. It was from the doctor's test. His handling of the sample was sure to be careful because of its suspect nature.

When I called his office at 9:00, the positive test result was confirmed. I was as ready for it as you can be when you think someone will say you're going to die.

I've always believed that the Lord has all our lives and all the circumstances of our lives in his hands. In His providence, He had let me be exposed to this virus for a reason. But the mode of exposure had yet to be determined.

"We'll need to test your wife as soon as possible," came the doctor's request. I told him I would call her to arrange a time.

My wife was also prepared for the news. In the back of her mind, the blood transfusion she had required at the birth of our last child was already suspect. The test would tell the tale. We scheduled a visit to the doctor's house for the next evening. The doctor wanted to draw the blood himself to insure the confidentiality of the testing procedure.

I can honestly say that I went through the day somewhat physically sickened, and there was more to the sickness than nerves. During the past seven days, I had developed diarrhea and had tremendous stomach pains. Under the current tension, I couldn't help but wonder if this was one of the first symptoms of what the doctors refer to as a "full–blown" case of AIDS. Eventually I would come to understand that in the light of this knowledge every symptom would become suspect. It kind of filters your perspective on every-thing from the common cold to the slightest fever.

Part of the problem was nervousness. Every time I got near my office, my church, or even my kids, I felt a tightening of my stomach muscles and a tremendous pain.

I don't believe we ever fully understand the emo-tional ties we make with people. Many people who work in my office are Christians. I go to a church with hundreds of members. My three children with whom I

24

am in contact every day mean the world to me. The thought of any one of these folks contracting an incurable disease from me or from anywhere is so painful to me that it ties my stomach in knots. I'd much rather just disappear and go find a job in another city or even just die and go to heaven than to have any one of them hurt!

In any kind of disease scare there are rumors along with the truth. In this case, I had to consciously force myself to let the logical, rational part of my mind reassure me that it was safe for me to be around those I love and those for whom I have a concern.

If my wife was indeed the means for transmitting the virus to me, then we'd both probably had the antibodies for two years. I've worked with all my people for two years and none of them had come down with illness. I'd attended the same church for two years, and no one had died from AIDS, especially none of the people with whom I have regular contact. Some of my clients and even my pastor had traveled thousands of miles with me, yet there were no signs of sickness in them. Probably the doctors are right. It takes blood or body fluid contact with another person to transmit the virus.

But right now I didn't know how the virus antibodies came to be in my blood. So I worked through the day and then went to prayer meeting. I can honestly say I don't remember what the pastor preached. It's hard to concentrate when your mind is filled with uncertainties, but I knew that no one else should be able to read my "halo data" and pick up any problem. So, I smiled, shook hands, and tried to act perfectly normal.

After prayer meeting, I attended our monthly leadership meeting. It was one I think I shall never forget because it triggered an emotional response I had never experienced in my entire life.

Our leaders' meetings are different from most church board meetings in that they are characterized by unity and organization. Our men are divided up into groups representing the primary aspects of the ministry. I serve on one of the groups. Most of the actual business of the church is handled at the sub–committee meetings, not at the general meeting. It is more of a reporting session on what has been done.

The meetings usually last about two hours, with the pastor going through a number of areas of concern and various gentlemen giving reports. At the end of the meeting, as the last item listed on the agenda, the pastor has time to bring up anything which is on his mind. The last topic on tonight's list did not appear on the prepared agenda, but when he announced it, I know my blood pressure must have gone to 180/110 and my pulse to somewhere above 150. He told the group that we must come to grips with the issue of an adult or child attending our church getting AIDS!

To understand the heaviness of this topic, you must understand a bit of the mind set of right–wing fundamentalist Christians. The sin of homosexuality has long been one of those considered worthy of death. That was the Old Testament Jewish response to sexual immorality with either an adulterous man or woman or with two men engaged in sex. In our time, many pastors still believe that the only way AIDS can be transmitted is through these heinous activities. In a way, admitting that you have been exposed is admitting that you are a sinner of the worst possible magnitude.

Apparently the pastor had just read an article in a populist magazine about the "Coming AIDS Epidemic."

He quoted a few of the hysterical reactions that were currently going on—things like kids not being allowed to attend school and sections of a town being quarantined for AIDS victims. Some people were even run out of town or had their homes burned just because they had the disease.

I must say that in all my life I have never been as terror–stricken as I was when I left that meeting. A hundred unanswered questions flooded my mind. Would they throw my children out of the church's Christian school if they knew that their parents had positive HIV tests? Would the small town where I live run me out? Would I loose the equity in my house because it was "contaminated." Would my clients all dump me and all of my employees quit for fear of catching an incurable disease?

As I drove home, I cried and prayed and cried some more. I prayed aloud to the Lord beseeching Him for wisdom! I didn't know what to do! My emotions were in tatters! For five days and nights I had gone from rational reasoning to irrational emotionalism. And I was physically sick on top of all of that. My body, my work, my life seemed like they were falling completely apart. All that I held dear seemed like it would forsake me if this terrible knowledge was ever known. All I thought I had left was God and my family and right then neither seemed enough!

Praise God for a wife who is a perfect helpmeet. When I'm upset, she stays calm. She has always had that quality. Being of a more artistic temperament, I have tended to ride the emotional roller–coaster at times of stress. In her loving way, she helped me regain control and composure. She assured me that we would indeed get through this thing together regardless of how it came out. Together we fell to our knees and prayed aloud to our God. We rolled on Him our cares and concerns. Then we felt somewhat better.

Tomorrow we would see the doctor and my wife would have blood drawn for testing. We prepared ourselves for the answer that we somehow knew would come.

Lord, we really don't know how to pray right now. We just know that you love us and that you have promised that all things will work together for good to those that love you and whom you have called. We don't know what you're calling us to right now, but we pray that you will help us to trust you and that you will give us strength in all that is to come.

5

More Tests And More Waiting

I love the LORD, because He hears my voice and my supplications. Because He has inclined His ear to me, therefore I shall call upon Him as long as I live. The cords of death encompassed me, and the terrors of Sheol came upon me; I found distress and sorrow. Then I called upon the name of the LORD: "O LORD, I beseech Thee, save my life!"—Psalm 116:1–4

I never have liked cloak–and–dagger games. I guess it's the plain upbringing of my rather common ancestors that makes me want to know people as they really are. Like that television show of several years ago, I always like to deal with "Real People." That's why all this sneaking around and hiding bothered me a great deal.

I believe Christians should be open and honest in their lifestyle. When Christians have problems, they share them, pray over them, and work things out together. That's why God gives us each other, churches and Christian friends. But for now, that was not the better part of wisdom. Perhaps it would never be.

As we drove to the doctor's house for the blood test, my wife and I talked about the possible results. She was already feeling quite badly about the whole thing. In a way she wanted to know, but in a way she didn't.

In all probability, if her test was positive, the virus exposure was the result of the blood transfusions at the birth of our child. That would mean she would have passed it on to me without knowing it. It would also mean that the virus had not killed us in two and one-half years. That was about the only comforting thought we had as we again drove through the rows of nice homes to the doctor's house. As I drove, I couldn't help but wonder if this crazy virus lived in any of the people in these nice houses. It probably does and they, like my wife and myself until the last few days, probably don't even know it.

The doctor met us at the door and ushered us in. He asked me how I was "holding up." I could have told him about all the things that had run through my head since Saturday. I could have informed him about the Wednesday night prayer meeting and leaders' meeting and my emotional episode coming home, but I didn't. I refrained because I didn't know the man's spiritual state. So what if the Lord takes me home at a seemingly early age? So what if I die, "before my time"? Like the apostle Paul, I believe it can only be better to be with the Lord. When my wife and I talked with our family doctor (a former missionary doctor) earlier that week, we talked about witnessing to this man, so our intent was to try to build a relationship and represent our Lord well.

The young doctor apologized to my wife for bringing this thing into our lives. His responsibility was to oversee the community blood bank, but it was not the blood bank that had done this thing, it was God. In His purpose, and for some reason not entirely known, He had allowed this to happen.

The doctor said that the results would be available at 3 p.m. the next day—Friday. Less than a week had passed, but it seemed like an eternity.

Friday morning I went to work as usual, and I had a great deal to do. Somehow, work has a way of allowing me to lose myself in the involvement of the moment. The business moves fast, and Friday was another very busy day. My computer hummed as I turned out a great deal of work for the company.

My dear wife had taken our car to the dealer for some minor warranty repair work. They said it would only take an hour, but because the factory had put some screws in too tightly, that one hour stretched into three then four, then six. Of all the places to get the news that you have contracted a life–threatening disease, the waiting room of an old car dealership is not the best. But that's where my poor wife got the news that her test was positive.

When she called me, I could tell she was quite shaken. I arranged to meet her as quickly as possible and we went out to supper.

As we looked at our three beautiful children sitting across the table from us eating a quiet supper, I'm sure similar thoughts went through our minds. Will we see them grown? Will they make it that far? Especially the little one. She's such a cutie—blond hair, blue eyes, and as cheerful as any sparrow you've ever seen.

My heart welled up with emotion at the thought of our being apart. The pain of the thoughts of not being with them and of them not having a daddy—or now a mommy—have been the hardest part of this entire ordeal to cope with. But the Lord gave these kids to us. I must consign myself to the fact that they are His, and so am I, and so is my wife. The Scripture is clear that he is a "special father" to the fatherless. My will would have me be by their side always. But His will must be my desire for my life and theirs.

It's amazing how all the other things in life pale into utter insignificance in the face of being with the ones you love. God's finest gift has to be a Christian wife and praiseworthy, obedient, loving children. I would gladly die in place of any of them. But one thing is for sure, we'll all be together in heaven for all eternity regardless of how long we have together down here. There was some comfort in that thought. And so, in my heart, I prayed:

Lord help me to take comfort in your providence and loving kindness. It's not the dying part that is bothering me right now, it's the living. Right now I don't know whether the shadow I'm experiencing is a coming tumult or the shadow of your hand poised to stroke some of your loved ones in loving care. Give me patience and grace until I know which it is.

6

Feeling Better For Now

Bless the LORD, O my soul; and all that is within me, bless His holy name. Bless the LORD, O my soul, and forget none of His benefits; who pardons all your iniquities; who heals all your diseases.— Psalm 103:1–3

I've always been a fighter. I like the challenge of being able to outdo someone else, not for anything like the perverse and prideful feeling of being better than them, but just for the sake of competition and accomplishment.

Knowing that my wife and I both have been exposed to a virus that could result in incurable disease brings out a number of different responses in me at different times. Anger, despair, hope, and worry are all a part of the emotions of something like this. One of the first reactions is to fight.

But how do you fight an enemy you can't see? And how do you persevere against something that from the standpoint of generating negative feelings can wear you down so badly?

I decided to find out everything I could about the immune system and how to keep it strong.

We live in a wonderful time of knowledge availability. As I understand it, the amount of knowledge in the world is doubling every ten years or less. So finding basic information on the immune system was as easy as walking down the street to my favorite bookstore and looking in the health section.

One of the interesting titles I ran across first was *How to Protect Your Family from the Coming AIDS Crisis*. Just scanning the book was terribly disturbing due to its presentation of no hope and a lot of hysterical data. Needless to say, I didn't buy it. But I couldn't help but think how ludicrous the very title of the book was. Right now it is estimated that more than two and a half million people have already been exposed to the virus and most don't even know it. "Protecting" oneself from it will probably become more and more difficult or even impossible.

One of the most popular diet books deals with building up our immunity simply by watching what we eat. Dr. Stuart M. Berger, M.D., the author, has a writing style a lot like mine—down to earth. I enjoyed reading his book, *Dr. Berger's Immune Power Diet*, simply from the standpoint of the helpful information he gives on the immune system. I must confess, I never knew just how marvelous this part of the Creator's work was.

Here are some of the facts Dr. Berger presents:

The immune system is the body's defender that tracks down and destroys biological troublemakers before they do us in. These troublemakers can include germs, viruses, fungi, and even cancer cells.

There are four key parts to the immune system including the thymus, the T cells or lymphocytes, antibodies, and macrophages or scavenger cells.

There are about a trillion (1,000,000,000,000) lymphocytes in your body. About a million of them are created or destroyed every ten seconds.

Lymphocytes are turned into supercharged fighting cells called T cells by the thymus—a small organ at the base of the brain. These cells can distinguish the good cells in our body from the bad ones which they attack.

When a foreign virus comes into your body, the T cells sound an alarm and new T cells are reproduced to outnumber the attacker, surround the cell, and release deadly chemicals that destroy the invader.

The antibodies are programmed to surround the invader and hold on to it while the destruction process is going on. That's where the macrophages come in. They are a kind of white blood cell that comes in, finds something covered with antibody, and literally eats up the invader.

The Scripture tells us that we are "fearfully and wonderfully" made. After reading Dr. Berger's book, I was even more strongly persuaded of that very fact. According to the doctor, our bodies are producing more than 200,000 new immune cells every second of our lives—literally millions of new ones every day.

Just imagine what would happen if our bodies didn't make that vital exchange on a regular basis? Truly it is the hand of God that keeps us all alive by His power. If our immune systems get out of whack, even for a little while, there can be tremendous complications. Cancer, colds, flu, and AIDS are just a few of the things that our bodies would be open to if it were not for the sustaining hand of Almighty God and His wonderful design of these things we call our bodies.

Finding this data helped me understand how crucially God's power is needed to sustain my life everyday. I may have never realized that had it not been for the virus he sent my way. My resolve is to do that which will keep my immune system in peak operating condition. That's not an easy task for someone who is a hard driver like me. I've always pushed my body right to the edge of ill health in pursuit of achievement. I've always prided myself in an ability to out–distance my competitors simply by "going the extra mile" and taking the toll physically. Since my teen years, I've always allowed myself to use a "run, run, run, then crash for a while" policy of taking care of myself. These modes of thinking were now going to have to change if I was to keep my body strong.

But I guess the most disturbing thought was that, for a time at least, that was all my wife and I could do.

Isn't it amazing how God brings you to places in your life where all you can do is rely on Him? Sure, we pay lip service to the concept all the time, but do we really do it? No, most of us don't. We all think of ourselves as being somewhat immortal. After all, don't we already possess eternal life? Yes, it's true that we do. However, in His wisdom and good favor, every now and then God reminds us just how weak and puny we really are. He takes out the heavenly ball bat and hits us over the head to get our attention, and He says,

> *"Be still, and know that I am God"* (Ps. 46:10 KJV).
> *I made you. I love you. I'm the one who is sustaining you every day of your life and for an eternity beyond that. Don't believe that it is any other way! Just trust me and what I am doing with you for today.*

7

I'm So Sorry

The plans of the heart belong to man, but the answer of the tongue is from the LORD. All the ways of a man are clean in his own sight, but the LORD weighs the motives. Commit your works to the LORD, and your plans will be established. The LORD has made everything for its own purpose, even the wicked for the day of evil.—Proverbs 16:1–4

Medical professionals are an interesting lot. Some of them have tremendous knowledge of the human body and its workings yet fail to realize the work of God in keeping all things together.

The doctor who runs our local blood bank, whose job it was to tell me of my positive test, was quick to make repeated apologies for the state in which my wife and I found ourselves as a result of the blood that came from the bank. From our family doctor we understand that he has been quite affected by our situation, but he doesn't understand where we're coming from in regard to spiritual things. To him this whole episode is a human tragedy. How differently we as Christians have to view such circumstances.

God, in His providence, orders all the events of our lives. He knew before the foundation of the world what this hour would hold for my wife and me. He knows even as I write what our end will be and whether we will remain faithful to the end.

Yet the blood bank doctor felt badly about things. He also felt it his duty to trace down the four donors whose blood my wife had received after giving birth. The process was long and involved. When you consider that twenty percent of the U.S. population moves each year and that the event we're talking about occurred two and one-half years before, the probability of finding these people was less than promising. After scores and scores of phone calls, however, all the donors were tracked down and found. Three of them were symptom free. One was not. When contacted, he freely admitted that he had a positive HIV result. The source of our exposure had finally been confirmed without a shadow of doubt.

From a human standpoint it would be easy to feel anger toward the individual who gave the blood. It would be easy to view his action as one that messed up the lives of people whom he never knew and to view it as unfair, malicious, and evil. It would be easy to blame God for not protecting His children who are trying to serve Him. It would be only human to ask, "Why us, why now, why not someone else who 'deserves' it?" But none of those reactions are proper. The reasons are simple.

There is not one of us who does not deserve death for the sins we've committed. There is not one of us who deserves anything but hell and the flames. There is not one of us who does not deserve to reap the consequences of our sinful minds and hearts. (As the sage has put it, sin would have few takers if its consequences were immediately meted out.)

Of course, we don't even know who the donor is. But we know that God is in control of all our circumstances including those that led to this event.

In our human wisdom, my wife and I had questions about whether we should have had our last child. We now know, as a result of the delivery of that child, that my dear wife could have never delivered a child normally. Caesarian section was the only option, and that usually means receipt of blood due to the losses incurred during surgery. Had we known that earlier, we would probably have taken more definite steps to make sure that two would have been our "full quiver." But in God's plan, even after we had taken proper precautions, He brought this little one into our lives.

As I look at my little girl so cute and perky, I realize that she has no idea of what went on around the time of her birth. She has no idea of the potential problems that we face now and that, perhaps, she faces in the future (it is still unclear whether HIV can be transmitted through mother's milk).

Right now all she knows is that she has a mommy and daddy who love her, and that she loves them in return. How great a lesson that should be to us at this time and to all God's children. He knows all about our tomorrows. He knows about the sorrows that are appointed for us, and He knows about the joys. Most importantly, He knows the proper mix of these elements that our lives need for our own sanctification and growth and especially for His own glory.

Yes, there is a lesson in my little girl's attitude toward her mom and dad who are going through a crisis now. The lesson is one of trust and faith in He who knows so much more about what we need in all the circumstances of our lives and beyond.

These events all underline the biblical truth that the sins of other people even unknown to us can and do affect our lives. God controls all the interactions of our lives—from when and to whom we are born, to all our "accidents," to our families and their continuance. Yes, even to our dying moments and beyond, our God is in control and He is orchestrating all of our lives for his own glory.

> If we could see if we could know we
> often say
> But God in love a veil does throw
> across our way
> We cannot see what lies before and so
> we cling to Him the more.
> He leads us e're this life is o'er
> Trust and obey, yes, trust and obey.
> —Anonymous

8

A Day At The Dentist

Heed instruction and be wise, and do not neglect it.—Proverbs 8:33

I've traveled to large cities like New York, Dallas, and Los Angeles. I've seen how detached people get when they choose to spend their lives in a large metropolitan setting where they know a few people at work, even fewer in the building where they live, and only as many as they choose to know beyond that point.

Small towns like ours are not like that. You get to know people—the doctor, the dentist, the fellow who runs the gas station, and the paper boy (or girl).

When the national media highlight a story like the AIDS epidemic, folks in a small town like ours react differently than those in large cities where they don't know who they are dealing with on a daily basis.

Their reactions are most interesting when you talk to them about things that are happening in the big city. They are, they believe, removed from the possibility of anything as hideous as AIDS touching them. If they only knew the truth of the matter! One of my wife's recent dental appointments is a case in point.

We go to an old–fashioned dentist. His office is in his house on the main street of town right across from the funeral home. He's been there for years. His office reminds me of the dentist's office I went to as a child and even his fees reflect the small town, "I've–been–here–all–my–life" attitude. Seven dollars will get you a filling. Or, if you need X rays, cleanings and examinations for yourself and two kids you can still do it all for $25. In some ways it's remarkable that the man is still in business at those rates. But his overhead is small, his house is probably paid for, and he is enjoying life.

When my wife went for what was to be her last time to visit him, she asked the doctor if he ever wore gloves when he worked on patients and if he had a fear of catching anything from his patients. His vociferous response was that he didn't even know anyone who had AIDS and that he didn't believe it could happen in our small town.

Being the concerned type that she is, this response greatly disturbed my wife. Only the fact that she shed no blood during the procedure comforted her in the slightest.

When I arrived home that evening, my first task was to console her after this experience. We immediately resolved to find a new dentist who wore gloves.

Our family doctor has told us how to handle such situations given the current hysteria about AIDS. You see, there is already a medical criteria established for handling people who have the hepatitis B virus. In reality, the hepatitis virus is more contagious than the AIDS virus, but there is no stigma associated with the hepatitis virus. In our case we should be handled according to the hepatitis B treatment protocol.

I detest dealing in subterfuge. It goes against all that I've learned and believe. However, until the hysteria passes, this is the way things must be handled. My wife and I both know this is necessary for now, for our protection and the protection of the medical practitioners with whom we come in contact.

If the current projections are true, small towns like ours will soon be unable to avoid dealing with the problems of the AIDS contagion.

A Wall Street Journal article projects the current victim number to rise to more than 290,000 within five years. In the absence of any know antigen or inoculation, the incidence of AIDS in small towns like ours will climb to what is currently the incidence in cities like New York—one in four hundred people. Think of that. Think of what it means to the church. It means that you will probably have at least one person in your congregation that will be infected by the HIV virus. Have you thought about what your attitude will be toward that fellow believer? What should the Christian's response be? (I'll deal with that question in a later chapter.)

For now we are thankful that we have no other symptoms. My wife and I are at a high risk, but only as the Lord directs will we suffer and die from this dreaded malady.

My morning reading included a passage from Calvin's *Institutes of the Christian Religion*. Here is a man who lived before any of our modern "wonder drugs."

I'm sure he knew of the ravages of disease in a more graphic way than we living in this century have ever known. His insights into God's dealings with men in order to show his mercy and grace are insightful when he says,

> To this purpose [the purpose of revealing the knowledge of God to men through nature] the Psalmist mentioning how God in a wondrous manner often brings sudden and unexpected succor to the miserable when almost on the brink of despair, whether in protecting them when they stray in deserts, and at length leading them back into the right path, or supplying them with food when famishing for want, or delivering them when captive from iron fetters and foul dungeons, or conducting them safe into harbor after shipwreck, *or bringing them back from the gates of death by curing their diseases*, [emphasis mine] or, after burning up the fields with heat and drought fertilizing them with the river of his grace, or exalting the meanest of the people, and casting down the mighty from their lofty seats;—the Psalmist, after bringing forward examples of this description, infers that *those things which men call fortuitous events, are so many proofs of divine providence*, [emphasis mine] and more especially of paternal clemency, furnishing grounds of joy to the righteous, and at the same time stopping the mouths of the ungodly. . . . The excellence of the divine wisdom is manifested in distributing everything in due season, confounding the wisdom of the world, and taking the wise in their

own craftiness, in short, conducting all things in perfect accordance with reason.

It may seem trite to say it, but only God knows what our future will be right now. I can take great confidence in the fact that it will be according to His perfect will, and I can know that this is one of the "all things" that will work together for good in my life and the lives of the members of my family.

> *O thou who art of all that is*
>   *Beginning both and end,*
> *We follow thee through unknown paths,*
>   *Since all to thee must tend.*
> *Thy judgments are a mighty deep*
>   *Beyond all fathom–line;*
> *Our wisdom is the childlike heart,*
>   *Our strength, to trust in thine.*
>   —Frederick L. Hosmer

9

The Bubonic Plague Of The 90's

Who shall separate us from the love of Christ? Shall tribulation, or distress, or persecution, or famine, or nakedness, or peril, or sword? . . . in all these things we overwhelmingly conquer through Him who loved us.—Romans 8:35, 37

It is currently estimated that the number of AIDS victims in America will swell to some 290,000 within five years. This will make it a disease of epidemic proportion. Almost every day, I'm hearing warnings from doctors in different halls of medical research decrying the fact that this disease can affect the general population regardless of its current concentration among the homosexual community. One doctor described it as, "the bubonic plague of the 90's."

According to the Kussmaul On–line Encyclopedia from Delphi Computer Network, the most severe outbreak of black death was that of 1346 to 1353. It depopulated large areas of Europe, Africa, and Asia. It got its name because its victims developed black spots caused by hemorrhages under the skin. About one third of the total population of Europe was killed by it.

The disease was transmitted from person to person by rat fleas. The two forms of black death were pneumonic and bubonic. The symptoms occurred suddenly with a high fever, chills, vomiting, and thirst. When swelling of the lymph nodes appeared, the person usually became delirious, fell into a coma, and died—all within a few days of the infection.

Because people didn't know how it was contracted, it was feared throughout the land. There was a lot of religious superstition surrounding the black death. People with black spots were shunned, as well they should have been, because pneumonic plague could be spread through respiratory water droplets (sneezing).

While the plague is still possible today, modern antibiotics can stop the disease in its tracks. However, the characteristics of it parallel the current malady.

AIDS patients who have made their case public are often shunned like the victims of the plague, even though AIDS cannot be contracted from a sneeze. And just as victims of the plague developed black spots, many AIDS patients develop purple spots from Kaposi's sarcoma. The most alarming similarity, however, is that a person can be all right one day, and in bad shape very quickly. In fact, most victims of full–blown AIDS die within two to three years.

I think one of the most interesting reactions to AIDS has come from right–wing Christians. They are very quick to condemn homosexuality, which is the scripturally right position to take, but they are also quick to decry this disease as God's judgment on the sinner. While that may indeed be the case, it should also be remembered that as a result of sin, many people who have nothing to do with the acts of sin committed by homosexuals may be harmed.

It is important to distinguish between a sexually–borne disease and the derivation of the disease itself. While the Scripture condemns sodomy—it was a crime punishable by death in the Old Testament—people who have contact with this sexually or blood transmitted virus will indeed come from all socioeconomic strata and religious persuasions.

Probably the most harmful aspect of the condemnation of the religious right and the equating of AIDS with homosexuality is the pressure placed on the federal government to give AIDS research a low priority.

Harvard law school professor Alan Dershowitz has called the posture of the religious right on AIDS, "An almost gleeful nastiness . . . 'I–told–you–so' gloating."

As Christians, we need to recognize that the church should serve as a refuge for those whose illness has caused them to be shunned by society. God cares for their souls. Repentance and a personal faith in Christ is still the best cure for homosexuality and all other sinful forms of conduct.

AIDS is a legitimate disease whose concentration among the gay population has made it illegitimate and condemnatory as far as the majority of Americans is concerned. As it spreads in the next five years, many who have never participated in homosexual acts, or who perhaps don't even know a homosexual, will be touched by it.

The taking of a cold, unfeeling stance by pastors who do not know the facts will make it most difficult for their people who are or who will be exposed to feel that they can continue their association with their local church. They will feel isolated, cast out, so very alone, and rejected. They will be under incredible mental pressure. Some will commit suicide. Some will just disappear. Some will die alone.

It was because of such feelings we eventually decided to leave the church we attended when this story started. We now attend a smaller church which has a very supportive leadership. How much better it would be if Bible–believing Christians could realize that "bearing one another's burdens," includes caring for those who are victims of this terrible nightmare.

> *If I knew you and you knew me,*
> *If both of us could clearly see,*
> *And with an inner sight divine*
> *The meaning of your heart and mine,*
> *I'm sure that we would differ less,*
> *And clasp our hands in friendliness;*
> *Our thoughts would pleasantly agree*
> *If I knew you and you knew me.*
> —Nixon Waterman

10

A Time In The Hospital

For I am convinced that neither death, nor life, nor angels, nor principalities, nor things present, nor things to come, nor powers, nor height, nor depth, nor any other created thing, shall be able to separate us from the love of God, which is in Christ Jesus our Lord.—Romans 8:38, 39

Being HIV positive, especially when you've done nothing to get that way, is a life–changing experience. Almost everything that has to do with your health triggers thoughts that are influenced by your condition and the cloud that hangs over your head.

Every cold makes you think about the pneumonia that takes the life of most AIDS victims. Every digestive tract disturbance makes you wonder if you're on the way to wasting away in some hospice. Every skin eruption makes you think of Kaposi's sarcoma and the marks of someone who is dying of cancerous tumors.

For nearly two years I had experienced painful attacks involving my stomach and mid–back. When I talked with my doctor about this, he ordered a battery of tests to be run including a series of X rays, an endoscopic exam, and liver function tests.

A small, non–cancerous polyp was found which the doctors characterized as "the kind of thing you'll find in HIV positive individuals." This was the first possible symptom of HIV infection. But it was not severe enough to warrant anything other than a "wait and see" reaction by the doctors.

Nothing else unusual was encountered. The doctor's diagnosis of my problem was irritable bowel syndrome. He gave me some pills to calm my digestive tract, but the attacks continued. An ultrasound exam was ordered and gall stones were diagnosed. Surgery was scheduled for a month later.

I can honestly say that I was more concerned about possible breaches in security regarding my HIV situation than I was about what would happen with the surgery. But the experiences involving the people who performed the surgery were probably as enlightening as the procedure was helpful.

The first person we had to deal with was the surgeon our family doctor had recommended. His reaction was to be as kind as possible. He knew the risks and had handled this kind of case before. He quickly added, "We're seeing more and more of this sort of thing."

I'm sure that doctors and hospitals all across the country are indeed having to deal with people like us. During the period from 1980 to 1985 when comprehensive screening was put into place at blood banks across the country, there were bound to be quite a few transfusions of contaminated blood products. Some of these people are still alive like we are, and they will continue to have non–HIV related medical needs such as gall bladder surgery. As of early 1992, 4,000 cases of HIV infection from blood transfusions have been reported.

Probably the most disturbing part of the whole process of going to the hospital and having surgery was finding a "blood precautions" sign posted outside my semi–private room. While I know that such signs are necessary for the protection of hospital personnel who must give service to patients, it seems like a way of broadcasting to all visitors that something is wrong.

My reaction was to determine that I would stay as short a time in that hospital as was physically possible to limit the number of visitors I might have and thus restrict the number of questions I might have to answer.

To keep from thinking about things too deeply, I brought along work to do. I was dictating reports right up until the time I was supposed to be prepped for surgery. I just wanted to get the whole thing over with and return to my home to rest and recover.

The head of the surgical team came in to speak with me the night before surgery. He verified that I was an HIV carrier and seemed quite uneasy discussing the preparations that needed to be made. When I asked him what was handled differently about surgery on an HIV positive person he said, "we're a lot more careful with things, and the clean up takes a lot longer." That part seemed to bother him the most.

The anesthetist was probably the person who showed the most kindness to me before the surgical procedure. She knew that a transfusion had created this problem for us. She knew I was somewhat scared. I could see compassion in her face and I heard it in the tone of her voice. I'm glad God sent her to be on the surgical team. He had been with me throughout my life and had not left during this terrible ordeal.

Knowing that sometimes people go "under the knife" for routine surgery and never wake up again, I prayed and made sure my "slate was clean" with God as I was wheeled into the surgical suite. If the next face I saw was the face of Jesus, that would be alright, too.

They tell me that the surgery was uneventful. When I awakened from surgery I was glad to be among the living. I didn't know what the Lord would have for me in times to come, but this hurdle was seemingly crossed.

In three days, I was ready to go home and recuperate. During the next few weeks things went well. I gained strength, healed up, and went back to work.

God had preserved us through the event and recovery. He had again taught us that He will be with us through all the times of our lives.

The soreness of surgery continued for the next year, along with some of the digestive problems. But it was obvious that God was not finished with us yet. We were still alive and symptom free some four years after contacting HIV.

> Oh rejoice in the Lord. He makes
>   no mistake.
> He knoweth the end of each path
>   that I take.
> For when I am tried and purified,
> I shall come forth like gold.
>   —Ron Hamilton

11

We Try The Alternatives

Then God said, "Behold, I have given you every plant yielding seed that is on the surface of all the earth, and every tree which has fruit yielding seed; it shall be food for you."—Genesis 1:29

I'm not a health food "nut." Quite frankly, some of the things people who are into "all natural" foods eat just don't compare with "two–all–beef–patties–special–sauce," etc. However, I'm not one who totally rejects the claims of those who use natural means to treat diseases.

Of the five billion people on this planet, some four billion do not have access to the high quality medical care we have here in the United States. Some of them make out quite well with herbal and natural remedies. It should also not be ignored that many legitimate medicines come from exotic plants and fungi.

The Scripture is clear that the herbs of the field are placed here by the Lord for the good of man. To ignore them, I believe, is a mistake.

In a nearby large city, we found a medical doctor who treats people with natural products and vitamins. Our reasoning for seeing him was quite simple and quite logical. Point number one: we put no hope in anything he might prescribe for us; we place our hope in the Lord. Point number two: anything he can prescribe can't hurt us and might actually help bolster our immune systems.

After a battery of blood and urine tests, the doctor recommended a whole series of natural substances for us to take. While the pills are not a problem, the Chinese roots we made tea from were so potent that we had to discard the plastic container we stored the tea in due to a bad smell!

Quite honestly, we can say that we have been overall more healthy since starting the vitamin program than we were in the years before. Yes, we still catch an occasional cold, but there has been noticeable improvement.

While most medical doctors would surely dismiss the whole idea of taking nutritional supplements to help boost one's immune system, our opinion hasn't changed. If all the vitamins do is give us a little peace of mind, they are more than worth the expense.

Those involved in medical science are quick to admit that they don't know why some things happen to the human body or how they can stop them from happening once they start. They are still trying to unravel the mysteries of the microbe. They are still working hard to discern the processes involved in making one's immune system fail to function.

In some cases, they are no more than educated observers that discover something and report it. They don't have all the answers. They don't have a one hundred percent cure rate either. The same is true for those who practice homeopathy. Negotiating one's way through the treatment options for a disease of this type takes study and patience. At this point no one has definitive answers, and it is left up to the individual as to which kinds of treatment he will subject his body.

My prayer is that both sides will recognize that they don't have all the answers and that they will work together to find them for the sake of people like us who through no fault of their own are thrown into a medical situation and quandary that has no clear cut answers.

12

When Someone You Love Is Suffering

Behold, I have refined you, but not as silver; I have tested you in the furnace of affliction.—Isaiah 48:10

It started as a burning sensation in my wife's face. It became a searing pain that encompassed the entire left side of her face. It was diagnosed as herpes zoster or "the shingles" in the common vernacular.

There was nothing she could do for relief. No pain reliever was strong enough. No moment was without pain. A rash developed all along the line that marked the nerve that runs through the face.

The poor woman dug at her face until she left deep marks on her brow. It was one of the most painful conditions in her entire experience. Recently a doctor treating her described herpes zoster as, "the scourge sent from Hell," due to the tremendous pain associated with it.

After several days of this excruciating pain, we went to the doctor. Not yet knowing that this is a sign of a developing infection, he prescribed Prednisone for her relief. Finally, there was some abatement of the undulating pain.

But this was not the first occurrence of this problem. Two years earlier—at a time when we did not know that we had been exposed to the virus that causes AIDS, she had a similar occurrence on the left hip and circling toward the genital area.

Standing by and watching someone you love suffer is painful. All through this ordeal, we have shared each other's pain. The mental pain has been the worst to this point, but who knows what the Lord has in store for us in the area of physical pain. We only know that He loves us and that He will take care of us. He desires things for our good and He gives grace to take us through the painful times.

Since Prednisone is an immune suppressor and does not really deal with the cause of the pain, the symptoms returned again and again for several months but in a much milder way. And while I know that the cause of all pain in the world is sin, I also know that seeing one I dearly love in pain makes me hate man's original sin and his actual sins even more. It is only through the blood of Christ that sin can ultimately be destroyed. Through the acceptance of His finished work of atonement on the cross and our coming to Him in faith can we find a healing for all our pains and sorrows.

Sometimes it is hard or even impossible to find healing on our own, but then many times the Lord brings us to a place of pain just to let us know that He is in control of all the circumstances of our lives.

Through all of our pain He promises that He will never leave us or forsake us. He will always be there as our friend and guide. He will always forgive us and heal our souls even if he does not see fit to heal our bodies.

Ultimately, when He comes again, the healing of the body will be accomplished as He makes us and our frail frames like His own glorious body. All those who have been disfigured by the scars of sin and who have cried out to Him for forgiveness will know the beauty of His forgiveness and the peace that comes after the pain is gone.

The night is mother of the day,
The winter of the spring;
And ever upon old decay
The greenest mosses cling.
Behind the cloud the starlight lurks,
Through showers the sunbeams fall;
For God, who loveth all his works,
Has left his hope with all.
         —John Greenleaf Whittier

13

The Diagnosis: AIDS

Whom have I in heaven but Thee? And besides Thee, I desire nothing on earth. My flesh and my heart may fail, but God is the strength of my heart and my portion forever.—Psalm 73:25, 26

It's been six years now since we contacted the HIV virus through the blood transfusion my wife received. Other than the symptoms mentioned in previous chapters and the gall stone surgery, we have been relatively healthy.

Recently, the doctors recommended that we start a program of T–cell monitoring. The procedure is simple. Once every three months, we appear at the hospital's blood testing center, have some blood extracted, and get a reading of how many CD–4 T–helper cells are estimated to be in each milliliter of blood. A good reading is 500 or more. A poor reading is below that.

Usually drug therapy is started when a person's count falls below the 500 level.

My wife's first readings were low—around 400. Mine were 800+, and the doctor immediately suggested that my wife go on AZT (Zidovidine) treatment. We decided to wait and see if subsequent readings were any different. After three readings, nothing has changed. She does not seem to be declining or improving.

With my readings at 800+, we were buoyed with excitement and hope. It's nice to know that at least one marker is positive. Then came the time for my annual gastroscopy to inspect the polyp discovered earlier. The results were to tell another side of the story.

For about a month, I had experienced some slight difficulty in swallowing. I didn't attribute it to anything but the irritation of stress and drinking too much coffee. In fact, when I stopped the coffee drinking completely, the symptoms disappeared. Still, in my mind, it seemed something was not completely right.

When I visited the gastroenterologist and mentioned the problem, I could tell by his demeanor that he was concerned.

He scheduled an examination for a few weeks later, and I went on with my busy life. Still the gnawing thoughts about a developing problem lingered.

Our family doctor had said since the beginning of our ordeal that he wanted to come out to the country and visit our home. When he called to ask my wife if he could come up on Monday evening after the gastroscopic exam had been performed on Friday, I knew there was a serious problem.

After the niceties were over, he came right to the point. The polyp now had a companion cancer. The facts were chilling. The cancer was in the esophagus and probably not in a place where it could be operated upon. In addition, this particular type of cancer has been seen in AIDS patients. More interestingly, four people have manifested this type of cancer and they have all been within this county.

Laser ablation of the cancer might be an option, but it would require the best doctors and techniques if it was at all possible. No one knew how long this cancer would last, how fast it would grow, or whether it would spread to the internal organs, but it could "migrate" through the esophageal wall.

Almost instantly, I went numb. The emotions I had experienced many times before as we had dealt with the problems of both my wife and myself came back like a flood.

Knowing the doctor's interest in computers, I asked him if he would like to join me in checking into a database and finding out what we could about other peoples' experiences with this. We went into the library and dialed up Delphi and the Computerized AIDS Information Network (CAIN). As we both suspected, there was nothing in the computerized literature about this problem.

We talked for about an hour about the Lord and how He does all things well. We chatted about the opportunity my wife and I would have to witness to the members of the medical community. And we prayed that God would give us grace to go through this part of the ordeal and perhaps even healing.

This symptom along with my HIV positive test gave warrant to changing the diagnosis from "asymptomatic, HIV positive," to "AIDS patient." Now the recommendation was that I, too, go on AZT.

Right then, we didn't know where this part of the puzzle would fit, but there was one thing we did know. It is something that I shared with the doctor from the Westminster Confession of Faith. It reads as follows:

> God the great Creator of all things doth uphold, direct, dispose, and govern all creatures, actions, and things, from the greatest even to the least, by His most wise and holy providence, according to His infallible foreknowledge, and the free and immutable counsel of His own will, to the praise of the glory of His wisdom, power, justice, goodness, and mercy.

Lord, I don't know what you're bringing into my life through these events, but I know that it is for my good and your glory. Help me to be, through your grace, ready for the challenges ahead and the glory which will ultimately follow.

14

We Tell Family

But as for me, the nearness of God is my good; I have made the Lord God my refuge, that I may tell of all Thy works.—Psalm 73:28

Our family is no stranger to the ravages of cancer. My grandfather died of cancer. My wife's father also fell victim to it. I believe that my father thought himself to have cancer and for that reason did nothing to treat the increasing heart problems that lead to a massive coronary from which he died at age fifty–five.

The two weeks following the cancer diagnosis were probably the worst since we began this odyssey. I can honestly say that I almost mentally came apart during that time. I cried daily, in private of course, and when driving down the road where no else could see, I often sobbed uncontrollably.

There are so many things I want to do in this life. Things that have to do with my vocation, things for the church and other people, and especially things with my children.

I turned to my Bible each day and prayed for long periods of time. I claimed the promises of God's Word. I played Christian music loudly in the car to try to program myself to feel better. But nothing seemed to work.

The thought that brought the most tears each time was of the children. Somehow I can't imagine not seeing my kids grown up before I die. As the older two approach their teen years, I want to "be there" for them. With a diagnosis of cancer on one hand and AIDS on the other, from a strictly human standpoint, it looks impossible that I will see them grown. My prayer has been that I would live long enough to see the youngest one finish college. Even that goal by which I would die at age fifty–six seems improbable right now.

In my mind and heart I know that the Lord is a special Father to those who have no earthly one, but I still have trouble letting them go. Truly, we are all the Lord's from the day we are born until the day we die. We really don't belong to anyone or anything in a permanent way, but family ties are among the dearest, closest, and most enduring on earth. To sever them prematurely before our allotted "threescore and ten," seems cruel and somehow not quite right. But then, we know that the Judge of all the earth will do right. It is in that thought that we must take confidence.

To this point, none of our family members had been told of the problems either with the cancer or with AIDS. But my brother and sister–in–law had moved into our area within the past six months to take a new job and it seemed inevitable that they would find out.

My brother is two and one–half years younger than I am. We lived in separate states for all our working lives. When he came to work for a local firm as a result of my drawing attention to him and his capabilities, I had no thought of involving him in our problems. But as I got to know him better during the first six months he was in the area, I gained a new appreciation for the way he had grown and matured. We share many characteristics and traits. We both like to make things happen. We both love our children and families dearly. We think alike in many ways and solve business problems the same way. And we have been growing closer over the years despite the fact that we were not that close when we both lived at our parent's home.

I determined it was time to let my brother know what was going on. On the next Saturday afternoon, I picked up my brother to go for a long drive through the countryside.

Because our wives had talked the day before, he already knew about the cancer problem. I'm afraid the information that we were HIV positive completely "blew him away." In fact, it took him and his wife three days to recover from the emotional bombshell.

I told him the story I've recorded here. We talked of our children and their need for care for the next fifteen years or so. We cried together, remembered together and laughed as we interspersed funny one–liners to keep the conversation from being unbearably heavy. All in all, he took it well. Yes, he cried for days thereafter, too, but the overall effect has been good. I think he understands in a new and living way the workings of the Lord's hand in all our lives.

Now I am seeing a marked change in his philosophy and attitude toward life. It is as if the information I brought was a bucket of cold water that jarred him into a sense of what is important in life. What had been an abstract tragedy that happens to someone else has now come home. His response has been entirely supportive and thoroughly Christian. He and his wife have talked with us about gladly taking over for us if the need becomes evident. We discuss long–term financial and estate details together. We spend time together each week and I know that we pray for each other daily.

There are times we want to let everyone know what is going on in our lives. The children still don't know. I would not inflict on them such a heavy burden. My wife's family still doesn't know. Why should they be expected to deal with this burden from a distance? My brother is here and can help us through this dark valley. But all of this cloak–and–dagger business gets old.

All my life I've tried to teach people how to live like a Christian. I hope I'll be able to teach them how to die like a Christian. But none of us is an island unto himself. We need the Lord to help us get through each day, and we need each other when the storms of life buffet us.

> Hast thou borne secret sorrow
> In thy lonely breast?
> Take to thee thy sorrowing brother
> For a guest.
> Share with him thy bread of blessing,
> Sorrow's burden share;
> When thy heart enfolds a brother,
> God is there.
> —Theodore Chickering Williams

15

Strength For Today

When my heart was embittered, and I was pierced within, then I was senseless and ignorant; I was like a beast before Thee. Nevertheless I am continually with Thee; Thou has taken hold of my right hand. With Thy counsel Thou wilt guide me, and afterward receive me to glory.—Psalm 73:21–24

Ten days after our family doctor had brought the word of the cancer, the medical people had done nothing to investigate possible excision methods. I was in Washington, D.C. on a brief holiday with the family, but called the doctor to see what was going on. He had delegated the responsibility to the gastrointestinal specialist who had done nothing. I chided the doctor and asked him where the "treatment team" was that he had talked about on the day he told me of the cancer.

As I walked the streets of the nation's capitol with my children, I remembered the TV scenes of several months before when hundreds of people with AIDS had unfolded a large memorial quilt. Outside I was smiling and trying to keep everything light. Inside I was crying and wondering if my name would be on one of the squares of some future quilt to be unfolded here.

Quite frankly, I was starting to "lose it" mentally. I didn't think anyone was making an effort to help. For the first time I asked the doctor for something to help my mental state. He had a strong anti-depressant prescribed for me when I returned home.

Within twenty-four hours, referral was made to a nearby large city and a doctor at a famous university hospital. An appointment was set up for three days later.

Our pastor and his wife went with my wife and I to see the doctor. Usually the drugs given as a part of the preparation for the endoscopic examination make you too woozy to drive. This means someone else has to drive you home. These people were all here for another purpose, however. While I was undergoing the procedure, they were praying for God's will to guide the doctors' minds and hands.

The endoscopic examination was conducted and a biopsy of the lesion was taken. While the pathology report would take a while to return, the hopeful news was that the lesion was in a position that could possibly be operable. The doctor would get back to us. The possibility of laser ablation was discussed as was regular surgery. Either way, it appeared that there would be a next step.

As we traveled home, we were thankful for the possibility of options. From a biblical standpoint, we knew that God doesn't call us through any valley—not even the "valley of the shadow of death"—without giving us the promise of His being with us all along the way. Right then I would have settled for a little bit of that daily "strength and grace to help in time of need."

Within several days, the doctor and I were conversing on the phone. He had called my office and then my home and left messages. When I called my wife from the car, she told me I should try to talk to the doctor. I called him immediately even though it was almost 5:45 p.m. (Sometimes that's the best time to reach professional people directly because the office staff has already gone home.) The doctor answered the phone himself. I was glad for news—any news—that would possible lead to my staying in the game one more play.

The doctor spoke candidly but with compassion. Yes, the lesion was cancerous. No, the experts did not recommend laser ablation due to the possibility of not getting all of the cancer cells. Surgery was the most sure option, but it was a huge operation requiring an expert. I asked the doctor one probing question, "If it were you, what would you do?" The doctor voted for the most sure thing—the surgery. It looked like, in the providence of God, surgery was the path laid out for me.

While I did not look forward to the pain or the recovery, I saw it as a chance to be with my loved ones a bit longer than if nothing was done. The next morning I called the surgeon the doctor recommended.

Often I marvel at the creation of God. Nature contains a million wonders. But above all this, God created man and endowed him with His image. The natural and developed skills he gives to physicians and surgeons ranks high on the list of things for which we should be thankful.

The surgeon was reputed to be one of the best in his field in the region. He was the head of the gastroenterology surgery department at his university. He was skilled in upper thoracic surgery and worked on the most challenging cases. Beyond all that, we found him to be a kind man with a warm bedside manner. He was surprised that the cancer had been found as early as it had, a fact that we could only give God the glory for. And yes, he could remove the cancer, but the rest of the esophagus should be removed as well to insure that nothing would spread.

The operation is called a "stomach pull through" in layman terms. The esophagus is removed as high up in the chest as possible and is cut off just above the stomach. The stomach is fashioned into a tube and pulled through the diaphragm for reattachment. Two incisions would be required—from the solar plexus to the navel and traversing the right shoulder from the back. The fifth rib would be removed to allow access to the chest cavity. A lung would have to be collapsed for ease of entry. Altogether, it would take about eight hours in surgery, two weeks in the hospital, and months of recovery at home. Not an easy scenario to play out, but there's nothing easy about living in this world. There's nothing easy about dealing with sin or depravity in one's self or others. There's really nothing easy in keeping time from taking its toll on us as we try to live out our allotted years. But it was a chance at going on. If there's one thing I've learned about HIV and now about cancer it is that buying time is what this whole situation is all about. Living today is all we can deal with at this time.

All of our lives are in God's hands. There is no such thing as time to him. He is eternal and unchanging. All He expects us to do is to use that time he gives us on this planet to live in such a way so as to glorify Him. Then in a place that knows no time—a beautiful place called heaven where there is no cancer or AIDS —we'll be in perfect health and enjoying fellowship with Him forever.

Perhaps this was not the time for me to go home. Perhaps God was not finished with me yet. I still wonder why He let us know of the potential problems before they were so severe as to overtake us. I can't help but think that He has several things He wants us to do for His glory before He takes us home to be with Him. Each day I must learn to be patient and trust in Him for strength for that day and each trying day to come.

Lord, help me to be strong for whatever you have in store. I don't know how to pray right now, but I recognize your sovereignty over all the events of our lives. Prune us, Lord, that we might bring forth more fruit to the praise of your glory and your grace.

16

Under The Knife

Because he has loved Me, therefore I will deliver him; I will set him securely on high, because he has known My name. He will call upon Me, and I will answer him; I will be with him in trouble; I will rescue him, and honor him. With a long life I will satisfy him, and let him behold My salvation.—Psalm 91:14–16

As the day to enter the hospital drew nearer, I found myself taking care of details that would be appropriate for a one–way trip. While there was only a projected three percent mortality rate with the operation and I had passed the preoperative physical meaning that the doctors thought I could handle the process, it was still a big operation during which a lot of bad things could happen. Mentally I looked at the surgery as another challenge that would have to be met. Physically I had little reason to doubt I could make it barring most circumstances except maybe a heart attack.

The major thought with which I had to come to grips was that of being totally in someone else's care and not knowing what was going on with my life for a period of days or weeks. But I knew I wanted to live. I wanted to be with my wife and children. I wanted to serve God with my life.

We arrived at the hospital on Sunday afternoon. After check in, we were shown to a room. Almost immediately, the nurses started the preparation process—an IV needle was inserted in my arm and preoperative antibiotics were started along with glucose. A surgical scrub was given me with instructions to shower and remove the bacteria on the skin, etc., etc.

Surgery was scheduled to start at 6:30 the next morning. It would last a minimum of eight hours. (In reality it lasted ten.) When a heart by-pass or valve replacement can be performed in less than an hour of actual surgery, you can get an idea of the complexity of this procedure.

My wife and I talked with the anesthesiologist about 8:00 p.m. We discussed our HIV situation. Much to our surprise, we discovered that the doctor was a Christian. Her mother had died several years ago of AIDS—transmitted via contaminated blood. Wouldn't you know it, God in His providence had brought us someone who understood the needs of our hearts and minds at this hour. We both marveled at his leading in this detail.

I didn't sleep all night long, mostly due to my own apprehensions about what was to come. I can't remember a more miserable night. Yes, I feared for my life, but

I also feared for the lives of those who would perform the surgery. I prayed that God would protect them from the HIV in my blood. I prayed for the surgeons, that God would guide their hands.

As I said good–bye to my wife at about 6:00 a.m., I prayed that God would preserve me if it was His will. During the ride to the operating room, I thought about my beautiful children and my dear wife. How much we love each other. How great would be the hurt if any one of us would die. How much more must God love us! How much greater must be the hurt in His heart for those who die and spend eternity in Hell!

The last thing I remember was scooting off the gurney onto the surgical table and thinking to myself, "Lord, my life is in your hands. Not my will but Thine be done."

I didn't know how things would come out. Would they find more cancer? Had it spread to other organs? Would I leave the hospital and ever return to a "normal" life? I only knew I was in God's care and that He would watch over me.

I'm thankful for doctors and the skills God has given them. I'm also thankful for the medicines that exist during this time in history. For the most part, I do not remember what happened during the next three days. I've been told that I was in and out of consciousness most of that time.

Of the few things I remember clearly there was the brief visit from my brother and sister–in–law. I remember my close friend and pastor squeezing my hand and praying over me. And, of course, I remember my wife being there almost every time I was awake. How good God is to give us others to help us through the tough times of life.

81

Then there was the clock on the wall. For some strange reason, the clock on the wall at the end of the bed in the recovery room where I was staying had stopped. Every time I woke up and looked at the clock, it was two o'clock. Under the influence of the morphine, I wondered if I was going crazy or if time had indeed stood still for me. Eventually I was moved to another room with a working clock. It's funny what you remember when you're not in control of what is happening with your body.

The surgery was apparently a success, but the next two weeks were fraught with difficulty and pain. The medicines they gave me for pain made me hallucinate and see colored spirals and bugs running up and down the walls. But I was alive and recovering quickly. The nights were the worst part. The pain reliever made me hyper to the point that I could not sleep. One night I dreamed that I was in a time machine and that people were coming in and out of the room by the dozens. Several nights I imagined that there was a rally going on just down the hall with thousands of people in attendance. In my drug–induced state, I imagined seeing people as nurses that I knew from ten years ago. Having never "done drugs," I was amazed at the tricks they played on my mind.

After nearly two weeks of being fed intravenously, it was time to try out the new plumbing. First came the pumping in of liquid food through a stomach tube that was hung out of my intestines during surgery. For two nights a funny smelling liquid that resembled Metrical was pumped into my body. Of course, this was a test of the elimination process as well.

When it came time to try solid food, I was frightened at the prospects. I had survived the surgery, the removal of chest tubes, the drugs, and the sleepiness. Would the anastomosis (joining of the stomach and the end of the esophagus) hold together? Could I swallow normally? Would I choke? I started with liquids and things seemed to go down well. In several days, I tried some soft foods. I found out very quickly that there were major changes that would require getting used to. The new "normal" would not at all be like the old.

I could only eat the tiniest of amounts. And I no longer had muscles to push the food down beyond the anastomosis. The food would go just past the glottis and stick until washed down by some liquid. The first time or two that it happened, I thought I was going to die from the discomfort. Later I determined that the food was making large masses of mucous float up to the throat and that the mucous was really causing the extreme discomfort.

The doctor's staff team came in to see me every morning at 6:50 a.m. They monitored my progress and changed orders for me each day. The most joyous day was the one when it came time to go home. I knew that I still had much pain and many problems to overcome, but at least I would be at home in my own bedroom and with the people I loved.

My wife and I were able to leave the hospital on Friday night twelve days after we had checked in. The one and one–half hour ride home was one of the most painful parts of the entire experience. The pastor and one of the deacons from the church were there to help me up the stairs and into the rented hospital bed my wife had gotten for me to use. My children had never seen me so weak and poor–looking, but I finally was able to sleep that night. I was home and God had let me live through another round. During the next few weeks there were many times I cried uncontrollably when I held my children and wife close.

Thank you, Lord, for showing mercy to me and my family at this time. I don't know what the future holds, but I need to trust you in all the circumstances of life. Help me to resolve anew to glorify you with my life.

17

Weak, But Alive

For it is He who delivers you from the snare of the trapper, and from the deadly pestilence. He will cover you with His pinions, and under His wings you may seek refuge; His faithfulness is a shield and bulwark.—Psalm 91:3, 4

The Sword of Damocles is a familiar story in Greek mythology. Legend has it that a sword was suspended over the poor fellow and attached only by a human hair. If the hair were to break, the sword would plunge point first into his head. Sometimes that's the way my wife and I feel about HIV. We know it is there. It hasn't slain us yet, but should it become active, we would not be long for this world. Besides the occasional bouts of depression this phenomenon brings, we now had added to it the sword of cancer.

As I lay in my bedroom recovering, I realized just how weak a human being could get and remain. Just getting out of bed for a shower each day was major work. Because a lung had been collapsed, breathing was painful. Sometimes standing under the running shower I felt as if I would drown simply because I had so much trouble breathing. Then there was the continuous coughing which would not abate for four months. Cough drops helped, but for the most part, it simply had to be endured.

Eating was a different experience each day. Some days some foods would go down, other days they would not. Along the way I can honestly say I had no appetite (and I still don't). I started losing weight rapidly once I was home. (To date, I've lost 60 lbs.)

Eventually I gained enough strength to go up and down stairs. I would sit in a chair in the family room and watch TV with the family for a few hours each day until I had to lie down again. The recovery process was slower than I could have possibly imagined. I think I gained some understanding of what those who contend with long–term disabilities must deal with. The difference was that I knew I was getting better and that HIV hadn't hit me while I was down.

The visiting nurses that came to see me while I was recovering were kind and efficient. One of them was being regularly tested for HIV as a result of a needle stick injury in the past two years. She could empathize with our situation.

Statistics tell us that in the next five years, three out of every ten people will have someone with HIV touch their lives in some way. Whether through someone who has the virus or through someone who has a friend or relative with HIV, the experience will be wide–spread. This means that people who have not had to think about their reaction to HIV carriers like us will in all probability have to deal with that information and determine how they feel about such people.

Recently I was talking with a friend of mine in the Christian publishing business. He mentioned that he was working with a company that is publishing a Bible curriculum for Christian schools that deals especially with the ministry of the gospel to hurting people. One of the lessons asks the children how they would react if they found out that a person who they knew was diagnosed with AIDS. The next question was, "What would you do if it was your brother?" That's a legitimate question that Christian people are going to have to answer. It may not be a familial brother, but it will be a brother or sister in Christ. Cutting them off from your life will not be a demonstration of the love of God.

I wish I could say the recovery from the surgery was without incident. It was not. Several times, the mucous problems mentioned earlier resurfaced causing some scary moments. Once, a vitamin pill got stuck in my throat for two hours while I was home alone. I finally got it to pass by consuming large quantities of warm water. Some days I'm so tired that I have to lie down as soon as I get home from work or go to bed very early. The weekends almost always find me playing couch potato although my strength is slowly returning.

The specter of returning cancer now haunts me along with the fear of HIV. I pray and read, and pray some more.

Truly, it's not the dying part that bothers me so much as it is the living. I can see more and more each day why the Apostle Paul wanted to depart and be with Christ rather than to stay here. Yes, there is joy in seeing my children grow up. Yes, there is joy in seeing our church grow. And yes, there is fulfillment in getting back to work, back to helping people, and even back to working with some of my more hard–to–work–with clients. But the overall trend is only downward toward the grave.

I truly want to live for others and the Lord. In my humble opinion that's the only thing worth living for. And there's one thing more. If I, through my suffering, can help Christian people understand how to better minister to hurting people and how to help the others who will come after me with this malady, I will consider the effort worthwhile.

Lord, help me to communicate your love to a lost and dying world. Help me to embrace those who are dying today for we are all dying a little bit. May I, through your love and your Spirit's work help people to see that the person in the pew next to them may be just like me.

18

My Wife's Reaction

Trust in the LORD with all your heart, and do not lean on your own understanding. In all your ways acknowledge Him, and He will make your paths straight.—Proverbs 3:5, 6

I remember well the Saturday morning that this nightmare began. My husband was frantic on the other end of the phone line. He told me that the doctor overseeing the local bloodbank informed him he was HIV positive. I assured him we would get through this together and that I would stand by him regardless of what might come. (At that time, I didn't know I was the reason or cause for the situation.)

My next reaction was to pray. I asked the Lord to help my husband find someone to tell because he was so frantic. God in His providence allowed our associate pastor to be at the church where my husband could find him. His positive reaction was just what my husband needed at that time.

The following week when I found out that I, too, was HIV positive and had gotten the virus through a blood transfusion, my first reaction was to ask, "Why me, God?" And then He quietly taught me how to trust Him even though I suffered in silence. (In the past six years, I've probably read more on the subject of trusting God than I had read on all other subjects combined in the six years before that.)

One of most difficult areas with which I have had to deal is that of false guilt brought on by the idea that I had caused such a damaging illness to come to my family. The overall effect has been to make me hypersensitive to anything that even resembles criticism. I've lain awake many nights thinking about what has happened. I've practically worn myself out trying to realize what I have done to deserve such a curse.

When I read of Job's trials and realized how impatient he was when God was testing him, I came to understand that I was only human and that guilt—false or real—is a part of being human. I also learned that I could overcome that guilt through trusting in the fact that God knows exactly what He is doing in our lives. I realized that, in order to reign with Christ, we must suffer. That isn't easy for us to understand, but I as I experience it, I know that it is exactly what God is doing.

Eventually, I came to the place of asking God how I could best use this experience to help others. During the first several years that we knew of our condition, only our doctors knew of our infection. But doctors are people, too. They are the people who have seen in our reaction to this crisis our knowledge of Christ and that He is helping us through this. Their reactions have been positive in that they are glad we have a strong faith. Our prayer is that those who have faith in Christ will be strengthened by our example and that those who don't know Christ will come to know Him as we do.

Since we didn't know what other people's reactions would be like, and since there was a greater mood of hysteria in the country at the time we originally found out about our situation, we decided not to tell family anything. Even now, some six years later, most of our immediate family does not know what is going on in our lives. I still struggle with this issue. My mother is elderly, and while I believe she would react in a Christian way, I don't want her to have to bear this burden during her declining years. But I've decided that if I become seriously ill while she is still capable of handling the knowledge, I probably will tell her. In the near future, I plan on telling a few others in the immediate family. I'm sure it will be extremely difficult for me to tell and for them to hear and understand.

My children are among the richest blessings God has given me. My heart's desire is that I will see them graduate from college and have families of their own. They are one of my major concerns because I want them to become Christ–like people. So far, they're doing very well in this regard, but like Hezekiah, I pray for a few more years in which to help them learn what they need to learn. So far, they know nothing about our situation, but they know we've acted strangely at times. The oldest probably realizes something of a serious nature is going on, but does not know what. If they should have to know about our situation, I'd like to be the one that tells them. In time, we'll have to see if that is practical or beneficial. At this point, they need to concentrate on growing up, not carrying this burden. We pray for God's wisdom in knowing what is best in this decision.

One of the major comforts during this time has been the reaction and support of certain close friends. This is not information you can entrust to just anyone. Some people would react hysterically, others would not want to help. But the few close friends we've chosen to tell have been quite supportive in many ways. From just listening when we've been a bit crazy, to calling and simply asking, "How are you today?" to writing notes and dropping them in the mail, they've let us know that they are holding us up in prayer and in their thoughts.

Recently, I've started working with a Christian counselor. I would strongly recommend this to anyone who is HIV positive. He has helped clarify that I am not denying the facts of my situation, that I should still set goals for myself and enjoy living, and that I should watch out for stressful or unrealistic goals. An important lesson he's taught me is that it is good to continue helping other people even though my own situation is difficult.

Even though my attitude has not always been positive through the past several years, the counselor believes that my optimistic outlook is a factor in my longevity. More importantly, he is another person praying for me and with me.

Recently I went to my doctor. He is the same doctor who was in attendance when our last child was born and the blood transfusion was given. He has always been very supportive and he is a fine Christian. During my visit, he told me that I would eventually die of this disease. However, he couldn't tell me when.

The important point to note is that I'm alive today due to the grace of God and I'm well—asymptomatic. The immunological specialist I go to tells me my T cell count and white blood cell count are going down.

Whatever happens, I belong to Christ and he belongs to me. Of that I am sure. I also know that heaven is much better than this world. After all the struggle, I will see Him face–to–face.

> *Face to face with Christ my Savior*
> *Face to face—what will it be—*
> *When with rapture I behold Him,*
> *Jesus Christ who died for me?*
>
> *Face to face I shall behold Him,*
> *Far beyond the starry sky;*
> *Face to face in all His glory,*
> *I shall see Him by and by!*
> —Carrie E. Breck

19

My Brother's Reaction

The mind of man plans his way, but the Lord directs his steps.—Proverbs 16:9

A few weeks ago my brother asked if I would like to contribute my thoughts to his book about AIDS. After all AIDS is not just the problem of those who have the misfortune to cross its path. In many ways, AIDS is no different than cancer. A cancer victim usually has some allotment of time to make peace with God and prepare the family for the major life–change. They are visited by those who love them, neighbors bring back everything they have borrowed, and a genuine effort is made by all to prepare for the upcoming death.

Whether the cancer victim is a Christian or an un-believer has little to do with how society reacts and prepares for the end. With AIDS the social rules we all follow are changed; nothing is the same except death.

As you probably picked up from the first line of this chapter I am the only brother of the author. My life has been changed by my brother and sister–in–law's situation. The lives of my wife and children have been changed because of the AIDS virus. God sometimes gives us the ultimate of trials just as he gives us the ultimate love. The verse above (Proverbs 16:9) in one short sentence sums up how God can and will work in our lives. It has come to have special meaning to my wife and I.

The Family Structure

To understand the full picture of the relationship between my brother and me, we must go back to the beginning. We grew up in a small, lower middle class home with the necessary material items and a major shortage of true God–centered love. Our father would give help and support to anyone that needed it. He worked two jobs full time and was able to keep his family in food and clothing. However he was seldom available to give us the nurturing and guidance we needed.

As we grew to be teenagers we began to understand why he was always working—our mother had serious mental problems. She could spend more money than he could ever make and she appreciated nothing. We came to understand that life with a manic depressive mother meant keeping one eye on the door just in case she started to throw things.

Although Dad had mastered the art of disappearing just at the right time many years earlier, his commitment to the family and keeping it together was unbelievably strong. Still, it was always a special event when either of us got to spend time with dad.

We both have selectively forgotten many of the details of our youth. I am quite confident that as children we failed to develop a strong bond because we were each trying to survive.

Somewhere in our youth someone decided that we should go to church. After all, "It's supposed to be good for you," Mom would say. My brother and I found the Lord in those very early teen years. We were active in the small Bible church not far from our home. Several men filled the role our father was unavailable for.

Children often learn from their parents' failures, and in our case this is absolutely true. The values we learned were instilled in us by our involvement with Christian people at church as well as our Christian grandparents and one very special neighbor who watched over the children in the neighborhood. What not to do as parents was a lesson that we both seem to have learned well.

Through the years my brother and I grew farther apart, especially after he went away to college. Then career circumstances continued to keep us in different states where we could not develop a close relationship.

In 1988, for the first time, my brother and I were able to get both families together for a vacation trip, which was without question next to perfect. My brother had a business associate who let us use an outstanding lakeside home in the New England area, and the weather was great. My wife and I both picked up on the difference in my brother and sister–in–law. They had each gained a little weight and were in the process of re–evaluating their church and their relationship with the Lord.

My wife and I had always been much too liberal in our approach to the Lord, and this became a topic of conversation when we visited my brother. My brother and his wife both graduated from an evangelical college and served on the faculty for a number of years before moving on to start a business. After leaving the college environment they maintained the Christian path in which they had been educated. At this time we felt the change in attitude was just a growing period and we were very happy they were looking toward the grace of God and not the legalism of man.

The vacation event was the first time the two families were ever together for an extended period of time. It was also the most time my brother and I had spent talking since he had left home to attend college. We spent hours trying to analyze the family situation that we had grown up in and how it had affected the way we now raise our children. The true miracle was the way the children bonded. I would have expected some conflicts or at least some boredom with each other but these didn't occur. The children were like one big happy family, a perfect fit. They simply couldn't get enough time together.

Bonding between my brother's children and my wife and myself was also very strong. The Lord was preparing us for the future and we were totally unaware. I now look back at what my brother and his wife were going through during the vacation and wonder how they could have kept their smiling faces.

Over the next two years our families visited each other several times for long weekends or as part of a pass–through vacation. Each time the bonding between us got stronger. Little did we know that the Lord was preparing us for a new direction in the journey.

During the latter part of 1989 I was searching for the next career path that would challenge and broaden my business skills. After sixteen years with the same company I needed a change. My brother's family had come to my home for Thanksgiving and it was during dinner that I shared several of the business opportunities under consideration. After dinner he told me about a couple of upper level management positions at a company with whom he did business and mentioned that my skills may be what the positions required. Without hesitation I asked him to check into the opportunities for me.

After interviewing for each position, I realized that one of them seemed to be the perfect growth opportunity I was looking for. In January, a job offer for that position came, and I accepted. Within two months our house had sold at an acceptable price, and the buyer did not want to take possession until June, the month we wanted to move. This all happened in a depressed market. Every step of the transition could not have been planned more perfectly. My wife felt sure that the Lord was in control.

In the process of transition we decided against buying another home because the department in which I was working was to move out of state within eighteen months. Just as I started to look for a home I received a call from a person I had worked with in the past and he gave me the name of a friend who had moved and had been unable to sell his home. He now wanted to rent or lease. As it turned out the person who owned the house was the associate pastor who had counseled my brother in the early days of dealing with AIDS. He was one of the few people who knew about the situation. The house was very nice and the rent was affordable. It all went like clockwork. The Lord had placed me in a new job and provided a house. Everything was going well. It was just at that point that the journey took a wild turn.

I remember getting a call at work from my wife who asked if I could make a special effort to be home for dinner early on a Friday. I was able to get everything done and left work about a half hour early. My wife had been with my sister–in–law that afternoon, who had told her about the test results that showed my brother had cancer in his esophagus. She had asked my wife not to say anything, but she just could not keep it from me. My sister–in–law had said my brother would be down on Saturday to tell me about his situation, but I was not expecting what he really wanted to talk about.

During the five month transition, my brother and I had spent much time together and for the first time in my adult life I felt a true love for my brother and his family. A very special relationship had taken the place of many difficult childhood memories. When my wife told me about the cancer I felt the Lord must be ready to take my brother home. This would explain why the transition had been so smooth. The Lord had led us here to be the support for his wife and family.

The next day I spent the morning unpacking boxes and waiting for the arrival of my brother. I was confident the news would be there was cancer and it was not treatable. I had tried to think of all the right things to say and how I might be able to comfort him. When he arrived I met him in the driveway and we talked for a few minutes. He asked if I had time to go for a drive and just talk. I said sure and off we went. As we left my home and drove toward the local state park, he started to talk about the cancer and what the doctors had told him. I listened to what the doctor had given him as treatment options. As we drove I could tell that my brother was very upset and I still had not heard the bad news about his cancer situation. All I heard was the optimistic views for treatment the doctors had given him. The situation was serious but not one of doom and gloom. Then he asked me if I knew what HIV or AIDS was. Though I considered this a rather inappropriate question inasmuch as we were talking about cancer, I responded that, yes, I understood AIDS and that my wife even had a fellow employee with the virus. He then proceeded to tell me the rest of the story that is spelled out in this book. The next two hours were spent alternately crying and laughing at one–liners as we drove.

My brother had decided to tell me about the HIV situation because he felt the cancer, which was very rare and found in HIV positive people, was the beginning of the end. My brother made a point of saying that there was never a desire to bring this problem into my life and that he was planning to have our pastor take the children. He wanted me to be able to deal with the situation at whatever level I chose to be involved. He did not want me to feel obligated to his situation.

His courage reminded me of our father. Somewhere during the drive, my sister–in–law called on the car phone to see how I was taking the news. I had no idea what to say to her. All I could get out was, "I love you and I will be here for you!"

The return home was very difficult. We cried some more and when we arrived I hugged my brother and got out of the car. As I walked around to the back deck and sat down, I remember feeling the warm sun shining on my face. I would live and my brother and sister–in–law would soon die. I prayed for this to be just a bad dream, but it was not. AIDS had found its way into our family.

As I sat on the deck my mind raced through the many options to consider—the children . . . my family . . . they will need us . . . when will they die? My emotions and thoughts were broken by my wife asking how the talk had gone and if the problem was as bad as we had expected. I replied with the bad news and we talked for the rest of the afternoon. I took the same approach with her as my brother had taken with me. This was her life, too. The acceptance of three additional children and all the emotional baggage that this situation would generate for all of us would change life as we knew it forever. It had to be a joint decision with total long term commitment. The response of my wife was what I expected—she felt we would be the best people to take over and she willingly accepted the responsibility the Lord had positioned us for. She called our sister–in–law to talk for a few minutes and let her know that the situation would only serve to strengthen our families in the Lord.

The next day was Sunday and going to church was difficult. Every word during the service took on new meaning. The knowledge of what the families would be facing made it difficult to hold back the tears. With AIDS you are forced to keep the pain inside, you are unable to reach out and gain support from your friends. I pray that someday AIDS victims will be given the same level of respect as other people with terminal illnesses. That afternoon my wife and I spent the day sorting through the emotions and planning for the future as we now saw it.

On Monday I met with my brother. Since I had several days to get my thoughts together, it was time to let him know that my wife and I were not willing to let anyone other than ourselves take the children. He sat down in the chair next to a display and cried. I was not sure if he was upset or happy, but I was quite adamant about the situation and a little upset that he had not directly asked us to take the children. Through the tears he managed to say this was what he and his wife were praying for. We both cried some more and returned to work.

The next few weeks were more of the same. My emotions were resting on razor's edge. Anything would make me start to cry. My brother had made the necessary plans for the cancer surgery and I was off on a twenty–two day trip to the Far East to prepare for a yearly new product show. I had planned the trip so that I would return in time for the operation. My brother wanted me to be there in the event things did not go well. I ran into some problems that mandated that I stay an extra two days but I would still manage to get home the night before the operation. Then, as with many good airlines, they managed to lose my luggage and make me miss one of my connections. I arrived home at 1:45 PM. With a few hours sleep it was off to the hospital where everything went well. The surgery was a complete success. The Lord had given my brother a little more time.

After several weeks my brother came home from the hospital and all seemed to be going well. However, the company I worked for had recently experienced several major customers filing chapter 11 bankruptcy, and I wondered if this could possibly have an effect on me. On the next Thursday I was terminated. This did it for me emotionally. I was beyond words. The pain was more than I could bare.

For the next two months I rested and tried to get my thoughts together. Was the Lord telling me that I am not supposed to stay here? How was I to support my family? The job opportunities in our area were few and far between. I spent six weeks using a career networking process to meet business leaders within our community and received three job offers all of which paid more than the job I had just lost. The people I eventually went to work for are among the kindest and most giving people I have ever met. The Lord knew just what I needed and He has provided.

I pray that the writing of this book will help other people who find themselves in a similar situation to deal with AIDS as we have been able to. As I reflect on the journey it is easy to see how the Lord has acted in my life. He has tempered and pushed me to the edge. The lessons have been well learned.

Our family will continue by the grace of God. You see, God never permits people to act contrary to His sovereign will. Consider the following passage of scripture:

Many are the plans in a man's heart, but the counsel of the LORD, it will stand.—Proverbs 19:21.

20

My Pastor's Reaction

He who did not spare His own Son, but delivered Him up for us all, how will He not also with Him freely give us all things?—Romans 8:32

I still remember the afternoon when Wayne told me about the presence of HIV in his family. We sat alone on opposite ends of a hard pew in the cold sanctuary of our church. I knew that something was coming, and I was glad it was. I waited with that sort of "nothing will surprise me, I've heard it all" approach that pastors soon learn to adopt. I wasn't shocked by what I was told, but I admit that AIDS hadn't entered my mind.

Our meeting helped put a lot of pieces together. I knew this family a little from their recent visits to our church, and I was growing to love them a lot. But they were a mystery. They would worship at our church, come to some events and then "disappear" for a while. They told me that they had been attending a larger church in another town for some time and I wondered why they were looking to change churches. I couldn't figure it out. Something brought them to us and then would draw them away. Knowing that Wayne and his wife trusted in Jesus made me want to give them space. I wanted to be of help to them but didn't feel that the gospel ministry needed to rope in saints from other churches. In time, the Lord would lead them to be more closely involved in our congregation. In the meantime, the elders and I lived with the mystery of the Marshalls.

When Wayne told me that he and his wife were infected with HIV, tears came to my eyes. I was thinking of the fear, the pain, and the loneliness they must be experiencing. How much the struggles and pains of life are altered by the knowledge that someone is with you, someone is on your side. The Marshalls knew that God was with them, but I wanted them to know that Christian brothers and sisters were with them, too. I realized that Wayne was taking an enormous risk in telling me. Probably he intuitively knew that I would respond adequately and would keep confidence. But there was a deeper fear that I might push him away. And well I might; I'm given to the same sins and fears of any man.

I recall the beautiful story in Mark 1:40-45 of the leper that Jesus healed. The leper came to Jesus and said, "If you are willing, you can make me clean." Those with AIDS are the new lepers. They are the unwanted and the untouchable. This is because of fear, suspicion, and disgust. The world—and the church— thinks first to draw away. The gospel is quite specific about the actions of the Lord. "And moved with compassion, He stretched out His hand, and touched him, and said to him. 'I am willing, be cleansed.' "

Wayne needed love, compassion, an outstretched hand and a touch. He needed to be counted as a person whom the Lord loves. He did not need people who draw back from him. The first and best help is simply sharing the pain. Since that first afternoon, my wife and I have often been at a loss as to how to help the Marshalls. When in doubt, we simply remind them that we are with them and will stay with them.

What things have I seen in the Marshalls? First, loneliness and the need to be loved. God's love to us is unconditional, and it is in that way that we love others. I wasn't sure what I could do for this man as he sat across from me (sometimes I still don't know), but I reassured him that I was with him no matter what.

The second thing I saw was fear. Fear for the future. Fear for the children. Fear of the reaction of others. Fear of discovery. The Bible says that "Perfect love casts out fear." The solution for the Marshalls was not to convince them that nothing bad would happen. Something bad had already happened! Nor was it to protect them from insensitive, ugly, angry or ignorant people. They can be found everywhere, even among Christians! What they needed was to be reminded of God's fatherly love and almighty power. Isn't that something they know? Yes, but each of us needs to hear that over and over again.

The third thing I saw was the delicate balance between faith and fatalism. I share with Wayne and his wife the strong Biblical belief that God is sovereign and that we are ". . . predestined according to His purpose who works all things after the counsel of His will"

(Ephesians 1:11). Further, I believe that "God causes all things to work together for good to those who love God, to those who are called according to *His* purpose" (Romans 8:28). But a funny thing happens when Christians suffer. We waver between a Biblical faith that says, "I am firmly in the hands of my loving Father and no one can snatch me away or do anything that does not fit his plan for me," and a worldly fatalism that says, "Heh, what can you do about it? You might as well accept it." What the Marshalls needed to be reminded of is that their suffering was real, that sin had brought terrible things to this world, and that their Father in heaven had given His Son to die for sinners and to put an end to the effects of sin and death. Their hope was not to think, "What can I do about it?" but to put their trust in the One who has and is doing something about sin. Fatalism accepts the way things are because there is no hope of changing them. Faith, on the other hand, accepts what God gives because there is hope through the Lord Jesus.

The last thing I noticed was the need for balance between being practical and being morbid. In our aseptic society, many of us lose sight of our mortality. Parents and grandparents slip off to hospitals or nursing homes to die, and we only see the effects of sin surrounded by flowers at funerals. We do not often live our lives with the thought that we may and will die. For those with HIV, that changes quickly. Death, whether short or long in coming, is a reality for them. That is a good thing for all of us to remember. That means many practical steps involving lifestyle, wills, financial and emotional arrangements, and long term planning. However, before this happens, life must be lived. Jobs are to be performed, families raised, games played, songs sung and friendships cultivated. How can we know when we will die? I have tried to help the Marshalls in the steps they must take to make adequate provision for all contingencies, but I have tried to keep them from being "walking dead." As the Lord gives them life, they must live that life to the fullest. It is my personal joy that He has already granted eight years of life to them. And I am willing to admit that my prayer for their continued health includes an element of self-ishness!

What can I suggest to you who read this? I am struck by the good that can come to the Christian church through the horror of AIDS. It comes down to this. What does the gospel amount to? Is it life after death through the resurrection power of Jesus Christ, or is it a myth? If and when Wayne's story becomes known in our congregation, many individuals will have to ask, "Is it only for this life that I hope in Christ, or is He the resurrection and the life?" "Am I associated with these people in my church as fellow 'club–members,' or are we bound together by the Holy Spirit into one body?"

To be united in Christ is to be willing to risk our lives for each other. I am confident that Wayne and his wife would give their lives for me; and because we are united in our common Lord Jesus, I am ready to do the same for them. AIDS will cause some with an empty faith to run in fear from a church that accepts such risks. That will be sad, but it will make such a church stronger. But for those who stay, we will have the confidence and excitement of following a Savior who loves us and has power over death itself. And we have the joy of sharing our lives with brothers and sisters we can count on.

My Pastor's Reaction

Lord it is my chief complaint,
That my love is weak and faint;
Yet I love thee and adore,—
Oh! for grace to love thee more!
                    —William Cowper

21

How Will You React?

Blessed be the God and Father of our Lord Jesus Christ, the Father of mercies and God of all comfort; who comforts us in all our affliction so that we may be able to comfort those who are in any affliction with the comfort with which we ourselves are comforted by God.—2 Corinthians 1:3, 4

A number of years ago, a close friend of mine came to see me late one evening. The purpose of his visit was to tell me of a sin in which he had been caught. As a result of that sin he would wind up losing his job and his provided housing (it was a part of his job agreement), embarrassing his wife, and changing careers. I remember well my reaction to his words. At first there was shock. How could he have come to this? Why did he do it? As the details unfolded, it was clear that some of the pressures on him were extreme and that as a result of them, he had been tempted and had fallen.

Beyond the initial confession of the sin and its associated shock came the working out of the consequences. Would I help him? Would I still be his friend? Would I pray with and for him as he tried to put the pieces of his life back together?

Knowing that there is no sin that any of us, given the right circumstances, could not commit, I was glad to forgive and help my friend. The circumstance became the turning point of his life. Today he is in a new job, has a large family, and is doing well. God has forgiven him and he has taken himself out of the circumstances that caused him to fall.

When someone you know comes to you and tells you that he or she is HIV infected, it will probably come as a result of one of two things. Either the person has been involved in sin—such as promiscuity, homosexuality or drug use, or has been infected through accidental contact with contaminated materials as a part of their job responsibilities. Either way, there will be a need for compassion and caring.

While I do not claim to be a psychologist or psychiatrist, it is my understanding that homosexual conduct is a learned habit—an acquired sinful lifestyle. As such, its remedy includes the recognition of it as a sin, the recognition that it is the product of a process of wicked thinking, and something to be repented of. My first response to a person who would come to me and tell me of their homosexuality would be to arrange counseling for them with a qualified Christian nouthetic counselor. Since the patterns of sin that lead to such a lifestyle are not instantly developed, they probably will require time to be reversed.

Another increasing possibility for HIV contact is among teens who choose to be promiscuous in their sexual conduct. Young people think they are invulnerable to HIV infection because they are young. They don't realize that when they have sex with someone, they are also having sex with all the partners that person has ever had.

If a young gal or guy "sleeps around," the possibility of HIV contact is greater. It only takes one sexual experience with an infected individual to pick up the disease. Once again, many of these folks don't even know they are carriers and many times no protective measures are taken.

The response in any case of sin is the same—recognition of the nature of the sin, confession of the sin, and forgiveness with restoration of the individual to fellowship with God. Obviously, I'm presuming that the people we're talking about here claim to know Christ as Savior. If that is not the case, acceptance of Christ becomes the starting point.

But what comes next? How will you react? What will you do to help the person in an ongoing manner? This is where your real Christianity comes to light. Your reactions can be one of the following:

(1) Reject the person immediately.

Unfortunately, this is the way many people are reacting to the entire HIV question. The reasoning is simple and fallacious. "If you have HIV, you had to have gotten it from sinful conduct such as homosexuality or drug use. Both of these are so repulsive that I don't want to have anything to do with you."

I'm thankful that our Lord did not react that way to people involved in sinful lifestyles. The woman taken in adultery and the woman at the well were both involved in sexual sin, but their belief in Christ resulted in His acceptance of them and their change of conduct.

(2) Conditionally accept the person but write him off over the long term.

It seems that Christianity today knows how to deal with the simple problems. Confess your sin, get forgiveness, go on with life, call me if you need something. We have a tendency not to stick with someone who is dealing with a chronic character flaw or weakness. We don't remember people who have continuous needs and check on them often enough. We don't take care of widows and orphans like we should —after all, isn't that what Social Security is all about?

The Lord was not involved in people's lives for the short term. He dealt with Peter's faults and temper for all of his earthly ministry and even after His resurrection. He had a special concern for the widows and orphans and their unique problems. He healed the women with the decade old problem with hemorrhaging (Luke 8:43–48). He promised to be closer to us than our own brothers and sisters (Prov. 18:24). Yes, while people with full–blown AIDS do not live more than two or three years at this time, scientists now believe that HIV infection will soon be like diabetes or other chronic diseases that can be treated with various therapies. This means that infected people will need our care and concern over longer periods of time. To me it seems like a tremendous opportunity for ministering the gospel to those who do not know Christ as well as the opportunity to show Christian love to those who claim His name.

(3) Accept the person as one in need of Christ's love and care for him in whatever ways we can.

I've never been divorced. For that I am truly thankful. People who have tell me that one of the hardest parts of dealing with it is the rejection that comes when another person with whom you have been intimately involved tells you to get out of their life.

In the current atmosphere of our country and its "grass roots" attitudes toward AIDS and HIV infected people, rejection is the major problem. Where do people like us go? Who will take care of us when we're sick? What happens to our children if, God forbid, both of us should become totally disabled at the same time?

In every crisis of this kind in the past, there have been those who jump in and volunteer to help. In recent years, however, the Bible–believing churches have failed in seizing the opportunities such a crisis affords. We have left it to the government or liberal, main–line denominations that have long since quit preaching the gospel to do the humanitarian work. Born–again Christians don't want to dirty their hands with anything that smacks of a "social gospel." Many times that includes not taking the initiative to use social problems as a means of reaching those involved in them with the true gospel.

One of the things I have tried to do throughout my professional life is to help those who have the true gospel apply it to their generation. The only way this will happen in the case of AIDS is for each Bible–believing Christian to realize that as they meet people who have HIV infection or any other chronic, life–threatening disease that, indeed, it could easily happen to them or a member of their family.

Many times Christians are philosophical and theological idealists. They think in logic–tight compartments. When they come up against something that defies logic, they conveniently duck the problem rather than working through it from a scriptural standpoint and administering the love and grace of Christ.

My own brother had to decide how he would deal with our situation. His response was totally Christian. He and his wife show their love and concern for my wife and me on an almost weekly basis. When I voiced concern for our children's care and future, he made it clear that he would be proud to take care of our children. He assured us that our desires for rearing them would be carried out including sending them to the Christian college my wife and I attended. Each week, our families sit together in church and worship the Lord. He is with me as I work with our attorneys to get our estate in order. And I know that he and his wife constantly pray for our situation. They speak words of encouragement and love.

Our pastor and his wife also offer encouragement. He and I meet once a week to talk about the current situation. We pray for each other and write to each other when we are apart for vacation or on business trips. His wife and mine walk and talk together and attend teas and Bible studies together. Such encouragement is invaluable as we try to make it through this life with a heavy burden and a smiling face.

The most important thing that someone who has been told they are going to die needs is indications that God's people care about them and their situation—even if they know that the ultimate end is physical death. As our Christian doctor told us one time, "We're all sinners and we're all going to die. God is the one that determines when and how." It's not the dying part that bothers me. It's the living I must do up to that point that is today's concern.

So, how will you react when someone you know tells you they have AIDS? My prayer is that your response will be in keeping with Christ's love for sinful mankind.

Lord, You made us all from the same dust, and we'll all eventually die. All we can ask is that Your love continually abide with us and that You send our way those folks that can help us make it through this troubled world. May those who call upon Your name and love Your Word understand their need to minister to their brothers and sisters and those who do not yet know You in such a way that Your Son may be glorified. Help us to come to understand what Jesus would have done in the situation and to do it for His sake.

22

How Will Your Church React?

And so, as those who have been chosen of God, holy and beloved, put on a heart of compassion, kindness, humility, gentleness and patience; bearing with one another, and forgiving each other, whoever has a complaint against anyone; just as the Lord forgave you, so also should you. And beyond all these things put on love which is the perfect bond of unity. And let the peace of Christ rule in your hearts, to which indeed you were called in one body; and be thankful.
—Colossians 3:12–15

Churches are curious things. In some ways they epitomize the best that Christianity offers. People that are compassionate, loving, and kind show up there to worship God together. Sometimes, however, they are less than kind, loving and compassionate. When a perceived area of right or wrong is involved, some church members have trouble looking beyond the immediate external circumstances of the situation to see the person in need of rescue or help.

The Lord was always compassionate. He looked upon the publicans and sinners of his day with eyes of love. He healed the blind and sick. He had compassion on those of low estate whose lives were a quagmire of sin and shame. From women caught up in adultery to men who were unfeeling and unscrupulous in their extraction of monies for the government of Rome, the Lord Jesus treated them with concern and a recognition of their sinful state and all that they could be to His glory after a salvation experience.

When the topic of AIDS is brought up in most conservative religious circles, it is more than likely associated with homosexual conduct or a suspicion of sexual impropriety. In keeping with the example of our Lord, it would be great if church members could see beyond the obvious death sentence and perceived negative circumstances from which HIV infection comes to the needy hearts of hurting people.

How will your church react to the first person in the congregation with full–blown AIDS? How will this person whose life is already in the turmoil that comes from a life and death struggle be received?

I believe that our churches will have to answer for how that person is ministered to. When we all stand before that Great One with whom we have to do at the judgment day, will we be found faithful in the ministry of God's grace to those who are hurting?

What can you do now to prepare your church for the day which will soon come in which you will have to deal with a person with AIDS? There are several things which should be the basis for our actions. They include 1) education BEFORE the first case becomes public, 2) counsel for those whose infection is the result of a sinful act or lifestyle, and 3) compassionate assistance with the physical, fiscal, and perfunctory matters which are part of ministering to the dying. Let's talk about each of these areas.

Education
Education of the congregation to the facts of AIDS exposure and infection is a starting point for informing your church and helping them to come to a scriptural position on this problem.

Rumors still exist regarding the spreading of AIDS by casual contact, through toilet contact, and even through hugging. I suggest getting a Christian doctor or nurse practitioner to conduct a Sunday School class for adults on the topic. If you have a Christian school, make AIDS a topic of a parent–teacher meeting. In addition, printed materials are available from the Centers for Disease Control, U.S. Department of Health, and other local sources such as hospitals and clinics.

Of particular interest to most people is the spread of AIDS among children. Special meetings with Sunday School and youth workers to inform them of the facts about AIDS and its transmission would also be in order. Most schools are now endorsing a policy of treating all injuries where there is loss of body fluids as if the person were infected with AIDS. This is a good policy since there are many AIDS carriers that do not now know that they have been exposed to the disease. I dare say that my wife and I would not have known of our infection until much later had I not given blood.

121

A certain amount of programming of the members of the congregation should also be the purpose of these meetings. Churches need to come to conclusions before the fact regarding attendance of children with AIDS, ministry to people with AIDS, and the degree of overall involvement the ministry wants to have with these folks. This will help defuse the emotional responses of the moment which may blind people to the facts of the matter.

Hysteria is not something which can be dealt with easily. Education before the first case darkens your door can help lessen the hysteria. Some people will still react in an emotionally unstable way. The church's leadership must recognize beforehand that some people may not elect to attend a church with an AIDS carrier and there may be nothing that can be done about that.

As is the case of any crisis, people's reactions will be all over the board. Some will show compassion and care for hurting people. Some will blast off in an emotional reaction that will not allow them to come back.

Counsel

Counsel is one thing which all people infected with HIV need. There is nothing like being told you are going to die to send you into an emotional tailspin. Several years ago when the general hysteria level in the country was higher, it sent a jolt of adrenaline into my system every time an anti–AIDS spot came on the television. Each time I walked into a bookstore and saw a magazine cover with large red letters on it spelling out AIDS, I got nervous and wanted to run the other way. Now, I don't react so strongly and instead find myself wondering how others to whom I must impart this information in the course of regular medical care will react. The last thing I want to do is hurt anyone or cause them to fear.

Those who do not know the Lord and who may come to your church in search of Him and repent of their sinful lifestyles will need even more counsel than your own members who may have this problem. If your church does not have trained counselors on staff to handle such a person, you should be able to direct them to a source of such counsel.

Regardless of their situation, people with HIV infection will need regular contact with compassionate people who can express their care and concern by talking with them, working through their fears and assuring them when they are down.

One of the most difficult parts of HIV infection is the mental ups and downs. Each minor illness can be seen as life threatening whether it is or not. Each cold or fever comes with doubts and questions as to whether it is the beginning of the end. Aside from the assurance of competent medical practitioners, helpful friends to talk and pray with are essential.

God has made us to be gregarious creatures. We need each other. Especially when we are hurting or in pain do we want to know that someone in the world cares about us.

I suggest a sort of Christian "buddy system" in which at least one or two other "healthy" people are assigned to look after the person with HIV infection. In our case, my pastor and his wife and my brother and his wife have taken on this responsibility. My wife and I can use them as sounding boards at any time of the day or night. It helps us to get through the rough times mentally intact.

Compassionate Help

Life is complex. Add together work, children, houses, cars, employees, and bosses, and you have a pressure cooker of activity and responsibilities. Throw in a serious health problem, and it is all a person can do to keep from collapsing under the load. The support that HIV infected people need is sometimes more than just words.

While the Lord, to this point, has not required us to give up our home, our job, or our children nor has He seen fit for us to spend long periods of time in the hospital disabled by HIV–related illnesses, others have faced these problems. Medical expenses, Social Security claims, and even basic housing are all problems which people with HIV encounter.

God's people should be ready to help those whose life is coming apart with the compassionate help and wise counsel found in the Scripture and godly men. Pre–planning your church's response to the physical and fiscal needs of a member with AIDS seems a smart course of action. Sooner or later the response must be made.

Start by finding out what services and help are available to people with AIDS from the "safety net" organizations supported by our tax dollars. Investigate what will be necessary to file for Social Security disability benefits for the person. Some AIDS patients have actually died waiting for the red tape to be cut.

Many communities are establishing AIDS hospices to take care of those whose death is imminent. Find out where such facilities exist and what is necessary to utilize their services if they are needed.

Consider establishing an AIDS support group for those who are infected. While most of the ones which are currently underway have a weak spiritual basis, it seems like a perfect opportunity for outreach.

The most important things are those which your church can do immediately, like caring and showing it to the person.

Recently a man came up to me after church. A fellow former cancer victim, he is now battling a severe depression. While he knows of my bout with cancer, he knows nothing of my HIV infection and the internal struggle and pain it brings.

After the man talked and asked for prayer, he broke down into tears. He needed to be hugged. He needed to know someone cared. As I put my arms around him and assured him of my concern and desire to see him well, he sobbed and sobbed. In that moment I believe we both gained a clearer insight of what God wants us to be and to do. We're to help each other get through this world of sin and pain. We only have today. We don't know about tomorrow or the next day. We could be dying or dead. We should do what we can this day to comfort, console, and care for each other. The Lord would have it no other way.

Lord, teach me that my pain can be used to help me identify with others in pain. May your church see the need to show Christ's concern and love to those who are hurting and dying. Help me to do good to those whom You bring into my life. For those who do not know You, may I have the privilege of showing them the way to the Savior. For those who do know You, may I have the strength to share their burdens and trust You for all the tomorrows. This is my prayer for Jesus' sake.

Epilogue

The title page says that this material was written by Wayne Marshall. The name is fictitious because I wish to remain anonymous to all but the few dear people with whom I have had to share this terrible story.

Let me assure you that the details are all true. Somewhere in this great country, our family is continuing to live out the story you've read here. We are daily trying to cope with the myriad emotions, fears, and frustrations that are the lot of those infected with the Human Immunodeficiency Virus (HIV)—a number which includes several Christian families who are not "high–risk" individuals but who are instead the victims of other malicious (or perhaps non–malicious) actions.

My wife and I don't expect to live long. Though as of the publishing of this book, we have been relatively symptom–free for more than eight years since our unexpected exposure, we have come to regard ourselves as "short termers."

Yes, we would like to see our children through college. We would like to see our grandchildren grow up. Only as God gives us grace to live that long will we have the slightest chance of achieving these landmarks. Believe me, there have been many times that we have identified with the Apostle Paul when he says that to depart this life and be forever with Christ is an option which seems attractive.

As Christians, it's not the dying part that is now causing us the most problems. We're ready for that. If we had our choice, we would probably prefer it be over quickly. Unfortunately, that is not the nature of the disease. The living is the difficult part. The uncertainty of the future that comes with this malady is a heavy burden. The concept of daily grace takes on an entirely new meaning in this context.

Our tenacity in living comes from the conviction that the Lord is not finished with us yet. This book was started three days after I found out the awful truth. That was five years ago. I'm thankful for each day the Lord gives my wife and me. As you've seen, it is logical to believe that my wife will precede me into the Lord's presence. We don't know. We just know that our goals are simple: glorify God, take care of our children, and help as many other people as we can.

As you think about it, please pray for my family. While I'll probably keep writing and recording the step–by–step trek my wife and I will make to the grave, it is my prayer that this information in its current form will help many people come to Christ and to a Christ–like position in their thinking about this dreadful disease.

If you would like to correspond with us please send your letter to the publisher. The business of publishing this book is being handled by an intermediary agent whom I trust. He knows my real name and location. He will make sure I hear from you.